I DIDN'T KNOW
THAT ABOUT
WYOMING!

D1531269

Books by Lavinia Dobler include:
A Business of Their Own
Animals at Work
Arrow Book of United Nations
Black Gold at Titusville
Customs and Holidays Around the World
First American History
Glass House at Jamestown
Great Rulers of the African Past
Holidays Around the World
I Didn't Know That!
It's Your World, Don't Pollute It
Land And People of Uruguay
National Holidays Around the World
Pioneers and Patriots
Rendezvous on the Wind: Plenty of Trade, Whiskey
     & White Women, co-author Loren Jost
When Greatness Called
Wild Wind, Wild Water

I DIDN'T KNOW THAT ABOUT WYOMING!

LAVINIA DOBLER

ILLUSTRATIONS BY WILLIAM J. LITTLE

WOLVERINE GALLERY
Greybull

The Cover. An original product of Wyoming; the sheep wagon. Still in use today, this is the sheepherder's living quarters on the range where his band forages. First built in Rawlins, Wyoming, about 1887, sheep wagons had large, iron-rimmed wooden wheels. Present day sheep wagons have wide rubber wheels, making them easier to move, while protecting the environment from damage. The sheep wagon was a definite advancement and significantly helped the sheep industry to become a permanent and stable part of the Western economy.

Library of Congress Cataloging-in-Publication Data.

Dobler, Lavinia, 1910-
I Didn't Know That About Wyoming!
LCCN: 84-62419
ISBN: 0-941875-12-1

First published: Selah, Misty Mountain Press, 1984.
Second edition, revised: Basin, Saddlebag Books, 1987.
Third edition, revised: Greybull, Wolverine Gallery, 1990.

Printed in the United States of America.
Third edition, revised
4 5 6 7 8 9 10

Published by Wolverine Gallery
P.O. Box 572
Greybull, Wyoming 82426

Printed by Pioneer Printing
P.O. Box 466
Cheyenne, Wyoming 82003-0466

I DIDN'T KNOW THAT ABOUT WYOMING!

Table of Contents

This Centennial edition is dedicated
to every Wyomingite,
and to those who find this state special.

PREFACE

In deciding on the questions to be answered in my book, *I Didn't Know That About Wyoming!*, I selected some of the facts that make this state unique, interesting and very special.

The selection was a challenge. There are more than 200 questions with answers — from the time Wyoming was a wilderness, then a territory, finally, in 1890, the forty-fourth state in the union and on into the Twentieth Century. I have also included several Indian legends and information about 60 movies filmed in Wyoming.

My grateful thanks to Steven R. Peck, editor of *Extra*, popular weekly section of the Riverton *Ranger*, for writing the chapter "Wyoming on Film," and Jean Brainerd, Research and Oral History Supervisor at the Wyoming State Archives, Museums & Historical Department in Cheyenne, who verified many facts.

The books I used most extensively were *History of Wyoming*, by Dr. T.A. Larson, esteemed historian who has served in the Wyoming State Legislature; *Documents of Wyoming Heritage* by Charles Hall, for the Wyoming Bicentennial Commission; *Wyoming: A Guide to Its History, Highways, and People*, Agnes Wright Spring and Dee Linford, editors; *Wyoming Blue Book, Volumes I, II & III*, and *Rocky Mountain Rendezvous: A History of the Fur Trade, 1825-1840* by Fred R. Gowans.

Lavinia Dobler

April 17, 1990
at Winged Moccasins
Riverton, Wyoming

The black-footed ferret, a member of the weasel family, is one of the rarest animals in this country. A small colony was found in the Meeteetse area of Park County in 1981.

FIRST, RAREST, OLDEST, MOST SPECTACULAR

WHAT WYOMING ANIMAL IS THE RAREST OF ALL NORTH AMERICAN MAMMALS?

Black-footed ferrets were believed to be extinct until 1981 when a colony was discovered on the prairie near Meeteetse in Park County.

This rare mammal, a member of the weasel family, has a long, slender body. With a distinguishing wide black band across its eyes, the black-footed ferret looks like a masked bandit. Its fur is tan, but black hair covers its legs and feet as well as the tip of its tail.

In 1986 after distemper ravaged the only known colony in the United States, eighteen black-footed ferrets were removed from the Meeteetse area to the Sybille Canyon Research Center in southern Wyoming. Since then the Wyoming Game and Fish Department has been engaged in a challenging captive breeding program.

Seven ferrets, born at Sybille in 1988, were shipped to the Research and Conservation Center in Virginia. Another eight were sent to the Henry Doorly Zoo in Omaha, Nebraska. As of June 29, 1989, 65 black-footed ferrets have been born in captivity. This brings the number to 122, with 57 living adults.

In 1843 John James Audubon, American ornithologist, journeyed up the Missouri River. While in the Dakotas, he met Culbertson, a British trapper. Later Culbertson sent Audubon the first known specimen

1

of the black-footed ferret. At that time, Audubon and John Bachman were working on the text and drawings for *The Viviparous Quadrupeds of North America* (later published in three volumes). The scientists knew at once that the animal was of a previously unknown species. They were the first to describe the black-footed ferret.

Long-range goals call for attempts to reintroduce ferrets to prairie-dog territories on the Great Plains in the next two or three years.

WHERE IS ONE OF THE WORLD'S FINEST FOSSIL FISH BEDS?

At Fossil Butte Monument, about ten miles west of Kemmerer, fossil fish are embedded in the almost mile-long low cliffs. Fifty million years ago, fresh water fish living in an inland lake were covered with volcanic ash. While working the Green River area in 1856, Dr. John Evans found fossilized fish buried under slate and calcite. Many years later hunters found a 13-foot alligator, a bird resembling a chicken as well as small fishes and plants. The 8,000-acre site was declared a national monument in 1972.

WHEN WAS THE FIRST GOLD MINING DISTRICT ORGANIZED?

On November 11, 1865 at what soon was to become South Pass City, the first gold mining district in wilderness Wyoming was organized. Then in 1867, the famous Carissa lode was discovered not far from the gold mining camp at the southern tip of the Wind River Mountains. Jim Bridger, mountain man and guide, warned goldseekers about hostile Indians. It's claimed that he said:

Fools and their scalps are soon parted.

Had Bridger been able to read, he might has been paraphrasing Alexander Pope's "Essay on Criticism," which contains the often-quoted lines:

> For fools rush in where angels fear to tread.

Seven years before the forty-niners rushed to California to find gold, a man from Georgia found some yellow rocks while trapping in a mountain stream not far from South Pass. Later he was found scalped, with a bag of golden nuggets hanging around his neck.

WHERE WAS THE FIRST OIL WELL IN WYOMING?

The first well was dug near the tar springs, a few miles south of Lander in Fremont County. In 1884, former miner Mike Murphy and his helpers, with picks and shovels, dug a hole in the red earth of the Chugwater formation near the Popo Agie River.

Twenty-five years before, in 1859, Colonel Edwin L. Drake had dug the first oil well in the nation near Titusville, Pennsylvania. The impressive celebration on Friday, June 29, 1984 at the Dallas Dome Field, the discovery site, marked the first successful oil well west of the Mississippi River as well as the 100th anniversary of the first oil well in Wyoming.

Union Oil of California continues to produce oil from the same field where Mike Murphy dug his first well. Although Dallas Dome Field was ten decades old in 1984, Murphy #1 is still producing.

Captain B. L. E. Bonneville, an American soldier born in France, in 1832 discovered the tar springs, located east of the Wind River Mountains, while he was traveling through this area. Indians had been aware for some time that the black springs existed. Emigrants who came West used the greasy liquid for medicinal purposes, lubrication for wagons, fuel and tack as well as liniment for their animals.

WHICH STATE HAD THE FIRST NATIONAL MONUMENT IN THE U.S.?

Located in northeast Wyoming, Devils Tower is a 600 foot-high volcanic rock. The monolith resembles a giant-sized petrified stump, and is the most conspicuous and unusual geological feature of the Black Hills region.

President Theodore Roosevelt proclaimed the thousand-plus acre tower the country's first national monument on September 14, 1906. In 1933, the National Park Service took under its protection a prairie dog colony within the Devils Tower area to preserve for visitors a typical Old West scene.

The huge tower was featured in the movie, "Close Encounters of the Third Kind."

WHICH IS THE OLDEST AND LARGEST NATIONAL PARK IN THE COUNTRY?

Yellowstone National Park was carved from the northwest corner of Wyoming, along with the edges of southern Montana and eastern Idaho. The largest in the world, the park has more than two million acres of scenic beauty: mountains, lakes and waterfalls. There are thermal springs and geysers, some 2,000 of them, and over 260 species of animal and bird life.

President Ulysses S. Grant signed the bill on March 1, 1872, to create Yellowstone, the first national park in the United States "...as a pleasuring-ground for the benefit and enjoyment of the people."

WHICH MOUNTAINS ARE WYOMING'S MOST SPECTACULAR?

The Teton Range in northwest Wyoming and southeastern Idaho is the most spectacular mountain range. The massive granite barrier stretches from Yellowstone National Park to Teton Pass. Many claim that the gray-blue pyramids are among the most breathtaking sights in the American West.

Spectacular, with no foothills in front of them, the majestic Tetons, covered with snow during the winter months, rise high above sagebrush prairies as well as the winding Snake River and glacier-fed lakes of Jackson Hole. The highest peaks are in Grand Teton National Park. The most impressive and tallest of the peaks is Grand Teton, 13,766 feet in altitude.

John Colter, a Virginian and member of the Lewis and Clark Expedition, was probably the first white man to see the awe-inspiring mountains. Traveling alone on snowshoes, he explored the area in 1807.

Wilson Price Hunt, enroute from St. Louis to the mouth of the Columbia River with his men in 1811, was impressed with the rugged peaks and christened them "Pilot Knobs." After they continued on to the Northwest, they crossed Teton Pass, which was originally named Hunt Pass.

When French trappers first saw the striking, pointed summits, they named the Grand, Middle, and South Teton peaks *Les Trois Tetons* (three pinnacles). Shoshone Indians called them *Teewinot*, meaning "many peaks." One of the tallest is still called Teewinot. The Teton Range includes part of the Targhee National Forest.

WHERE IS THE OLDEST STEEL BRIDGE WEST OF THE MISSOURI RIVER?

The old Army bridge over the North Platte River near Fort Laramie in the southeastern part of Wyoming is the earliest-built steel bridge west of the Missouri River. Constructed in 1875, the bridge was used extensively by the Army as well as by stagecoach drivers on the Cheyenne-Deadwood Route. Those who were not employed by the government were charged a toll fee.

WHAT FAMILY STILL OWNS ONE OF THE FIRST DUDE RANCHES IN THIS COUNTRY?

For years the Eaton family has owned the famous dude ranch or guest resort in Wolf, Wyoming. It may be one of the first guest ranches established in the world.

The Eaton brothers: Howard, Alden and Willis, who previously owned the Custer Trail Ranch near Medora, North Dakota, established their Wyoming ranch in 1904 at the mouth of Wolf Creek Canyon in the Big Horn Mountains, about fifteen miles northwest of Sheridan.

In the 1930s and 1940s, Western resorts for dudes were profitable for Wyomingites whose ranches of 500 to 1,000 acres or more were located in the mountains of the Big Horns, the Wind Rivers, the Absarokas, the Black Hills, Medicine Bow and the Tetons. Many ranchers are no longer in the "paying guest" business. They are concentrating on raising cattle and sheep.

WHO PREACHED THE FIRST PROTESTANT SERMON IN THE ROCKY MOUNTAINS?

The Reverend Samuel Parker preached the first Protestant sermon on August 23, 1835, a few miles north of the present town site of Bondurant in Sublette County.

WHAT YEAR DID WYOMING RANK FIRST IN COAL PRODUCTION?

In 1988, Wyoming became, for the first time, the top coal-producing state in the country, surpassing Kentucky, the long-time leader. Wyoming produced 163.6 million tons in 1988. This figure is the second largest amount of coal produced by any state in recent history.

Carbon, located fifteen miles southwest of Medicine Bow in Carbon County, was the first coal town in Wyoming Territory. Two mines opened in 1868, the year the town was founded. Also, this was the year the Union Pacific Railroad first went through the coal mining town. The peak year for coal mining in the 19th century was in 1888 when 347,754 tons of black diamonds were mined.

WHICH TOWN IN THE U.S. HAD THE FIRST J.C. PENNEY DEPARTMENT STORE?

Kemmerer was the site of the first store established in 1902 by James Cash Penney with two partners. Penney invested his entire savings of $500 and borrowed $1,500 more to open his Golden Rule Department Store in the small Lincoln County coal mining town.

Although there was competition from the company store where miners and their families usually shopped, the Golden Rule cash-and-carry store prospered. Penney later expanded the business, setting up stores across the nation, and changed the name from The Golden Rule to J.C. Penney.

Penney's modest home, where he and his family lived for years, has been preserved by the Penney Foundation as well as by the city of Kemmerer.

WHEN WAS THE FIRST NATIONAL FOREST ESTABLISHED?

In 1902 the Shoshone National Forest in the northwest section of Wyoming was established as the Yellowstone Forest Reserve. Theodore Roosevelt, one of the early conservationists, was president of the United States when the first national forest was created.

It was in this heavily forested area where Camp Monaco, "Buffalo Bill" Cody's famous encampment, was located. Albert I, Prince of Monaco, with Count

Beret, his aide de camp, participated in Cody's last big game hunt in September, 1913.

WHERE IS WYOMING'S FIRST NATIONAL PARKWAY?

John D. Rockefeller, Jr. Memorial Parkway is located in the northwestern part of the state. To the north is Yellowstone National Park and to the south is the Grand Teton National Park. Authorized in 1972, it contains more than twenty-three thousand acres, and is bordered with lodgepole pines. The parkway is a tribute to Rockefeller's role in the creation of many national parks.

WHAT ARE WYOMING'S OLDEST DOCUMENTS?

Petroglyphs and pictographs, found in many areas of the state, are the earliest known documents of Wyoming heritage. Years ago Indian artists created their symbolic art on stone. Mary Helen Hendry, author of *Indian Rock Art in Wyoming*, published in 1983, has written that archeologists call the incised, pecked and abraded designs petroglyphs. Abraded means the designs have been rubbed off or worn away by friction or erosion. Pictographs are line drawings and painted designs.

One of the best sites to see some of the Indians' symbolic art is at Castle Gardens, some forty miles southeast of Riverton, or about eighteen miles south of Moneta in Fremont County. The site where the artists worked is well named. The brown and tan sandstone cliffs resemble citadels of fortified medieval towns. Tall cedars, pines and berry bushes also lend beauty to the countryside.

Spiritual as well as ceremonial motives may have inspired the rock drawings, although there is still mystery surrounding the unusual artwork that includes the figures of hunters, warriors and many animals such as turtles, buffalo, elk as well as birds. Some eighty acres were set aside in 1967 by the U.S. Department of the Interior through the Bureau of Land Management to protect the rare petroglyphs.

WHERE WAS THE FIRST FOREST RANGER STATION ESTABLISHED IN THE U.S.?

The Wapiti Ranger Station in the Shoshone National Forest is about thirty miles west of the town of Cody. It was established in 1903 when Theodore Roosevelt was president.

Wapiti (WAH-puh-tee) is the name of a large North American deer, commonly called an elk in this country. Wyoming has many elk herds, particularly in the northwestern part of the state.

WHICH RODEO IS CALLED THE "DADDY OF 'EM ALL"?

Held the last full week of every July, the Cheyenne Frontier Days' celebration focuses on the world-famous rodeo known as the "Daddy of 'em All."

The first rodeo was held in Cheyenne in 1896, the event being a one-day affair. Now the festivities run for ten days, with 100-unit parades featuring century-old carriages. Also there are colorful Indian dances, chuckwagon races, concerts, carnival rides and an air show. Countless hours and talents are contributed each year by some two thousand volunteers to make the celebration a huge success, drawing large numbers of tourists from all parts of the world. Many observers, as well as Cheyenne residents and rodeo competitors, dress in Western clothing during Frontier Days.

HOW DID FATHER DE SMET DESCRIBE THE FIRST WYOMING MASS IN THE WILDERNESS?

The Jesuit priest, born in Belgium, who had been attending the last mountain men's trade fair, left the Green River (Siskeedee-Agie) Rendezvous on July 4, 1840, and traveled northward. Siskeedee-Agie means "river of the prairie children." His letter describing the service to a fellow priest in St. Louis was as follows:

> On Sunday, the 5th of July, I had the consolation of celebrating the holy sacrifice of mass... The altar was placed on an elevation, and surrounded with boughs and garlands of flowers; I addressed the congregation in French and English, and spoke also by an interpreter to the Flatheads and Snake Indians. It was a spectacle truly moving for the heart of a missionary, to behold an assembly composed of so many different nations, who all assisted at our holy mysteries with great satisfaction... This place has been called since that time, by the French Canadians, La Prairie de la Messe.

LARGEST, HIGHEST, MOST FAMOUS

WHAT IS WYOMING'S HIGHEST PEAK?

Gannett Peak, located on the crest of the Continental Divide in the central Rockies, is 14,785 feet (4.202 m) in elevation.

In 1842, Captain John C. Fremont, American explorer and soldier, with the famous mountain man Kit Carson as his guide, climbed what Fremont thought was the highest peak in the Wind River Range. At the top, Fremont drove a ramrod into a crevice for the red, white and blue flag of the United States. At that time the flag had 26 stars in a field of blue.

Carson and Fremont then descended the ice fields, heading for the Green River Valley, but Fremont soon learned that Henry Gannett had climbed an even higher peak. Fremont, who is often called "The Pathfinder," had missed climbing the highest peak by less than ten miles.

Two glaciers, Dinwoody and Gannett, spread in a fan-shape to fill the huge snow-covered amphitheatre on the north shoulder of Gannett Peak. On the south side is the Bull Lake ice field.

WHICH WYOMING FORT IS ONE OF THE MOST FAMOUS IN THE WEST?

Fort Laramie, the first permanent trading post in wilderness Wyoming, celebrated its 150th birthday May 30, 1984. This fort trading post played an

High mountain peaks in Teton National Park are among Wyoming's spectacular sights. Ranchers often build buck and rail fences (shown in foreground) in the northwestern area of the state.

important role in the settling of the West and is considered one of the most famous posts in America.

William Sublette and Robert Campbell, two early mountain men, built a trading post and stockade fort in 1834 on the Laramie River, about a mile and a half above its junction with the North Platte River.

Over the years the old fort, originally named Fort William for the senior partner William Sublette, served fur traders, wagon trains and the Army. In 1841, the wooden stockade was replaced and given the name Fort John. The U.S. government purchased the fort in 1849 for a military reservation, but it was abandoned in 1891. For fifty years it slowly deteriorated. Then in 1937 the state of Wyoming bought the fort and grounds, donating the historic site to the federal government.

In 1838 Myra Fairbanks Eells and Sarah Gilbert White, with their missionary husbands, were enroute to Oregon Country to Christianize the Indians. They wrote in their journals, describing the fort on the Laramie River.

> ...It is a large, hewed log building... A fort in this country is a place built to accomodate the Company as they go and come from the Mts. to trade with the Indians for furs...

Mrs. Smith, on May 30, 1838, penned:

> ...There are no Indians here, they have all gone to fight with the Pawnees. We are among the Sioux. We see some females of white men. Last eve we received a call from one of the wives of some trader. Her attendant said that she had never seen a white woman & came three miles to see us. She was dressed in fine style. Perhaps her dress cost 100 dollars... Her dress was mountain sheepskin, white & soft as kid.

WHERE IS THE WORLD'S LARGEST OPEN PIT URANIUM MINE?

There's a fascinating story concerning the discovery of uranium on a sandstone hill and the success of the Lucky Mc Mine in the Gas Hills of Fremont County, some forty miles southeast of Riverton.

Early Sunday morning, September 13, 1953, Neil McNeice, who owned the Riverton Machine Company, and his wife Maxine, a nurse, drove to Gas Hills by way of Moneta. Since it was open season, they would be hunting for antelope as well as prospecting for uranium.

When a few miles north of Gas Hills, Neil McNeice looked through his field glasses, studying the sagebrush and grassy countryside, and then at the hill some distance away from where he and his wife were standing. For some reason the mound of earth, sandstone and rock, later known as "discovery hill," seemed to have a different look.

Later, Neil and Maxine McNiece tested the earth on top of the hill with a geiger counter, the instrument they had used many times in hopes of detecting the presence and intensity of radiation. On that day the geiger counter went wild.

Excited, the McNieces collected samples of rock and sandstone from the hill before they drove back to their Riverton home by the Wind River. Neil McNeice immediately phoned Lowell Morfeld, his partner and good friend. He told Morfeld, who had been unable to go out into the field that eventful Sunday, that he thought this time, at long last, they had found rocks on a certain hill that might contain uranium.

Since that historic day in 1953, millions of pounds of uranium U308 have been unearthed from the largest open pit in the world, and milled from the Lucky Mc claims. The granite monument at the top of "discovery hill" is not far from the mine, which was named for the McNieces.

Note: This interesting account is from the article "The Uranium Story: Recollections of a Picnic in the Pit" by Roy Peck. It was printed in the September, 1980 issue of *The Mining Claim.*

WHAT IS THE MOST FAMOUS
GEYSER IN THE WORLD?

Old Faithful in Yellowstone National Park is the most famous geyser in the world. The geyser, which has an appropriate name, erupts about every sixty-four minutes, shooting 11,000 gallons of hot mineral water some 150 feet high above the nearby forest. Close by is Old Faithful Inn, claimed to be the largest log hostelry in the world.

The U.S. Congress created Yellowstone National Park in 1872 from an eastern portion of Idaho, a small section of southern Montana, and a large area of northwestern Wyoming Territory. The park has 2,219,823 acres. The world's greatest geyser area has about 2,000 geysers and hot springs. There are also spectacular falls and impressive canyons that have been carved by the Yellowstone River.

WHAT WAS THE GLORY HOLE?

One of the largest open pit iron mines in the world, "The Glory Hole" began operations at Sunrise, Wyoming Territory, in 1887 and continued to operate until 1974.

WHAT IS THE LARGEST NATIONAL
ELK REFUGE IN THE UNITED STATES?

About 7,500 elk spend the winter months in the National Elk Refuge where they are fed regularly. The refuge, which contains 24,300 acres of meadowland, including the foothills nearby, is located north of Jackson in Teton County. It's the largest national elk refuge in the country.

After the elk, in early spring, head for the mountainous regions farther North, Boy Scouts in the Jackson District, who have been granted a one-day permit, collect the large palmate antlers the elk have shed.

Later the Boy Scouts have the big job of bundling the antlers; then they weigh and tag them. An auction is held in Jackson, by the Boy Scouts to raise money for the elk feeding program. The National Elk Refuge was established in 1912 by an act of Congress, and is supervised by the Department of the Interior, U.S. Fish and Wildlife Service. Thousands of visitors go to the Jackson area to see the elk during the winter months.

WHERE'S THE LARGEST STEAM LOCOMOTIVE IN THE WORLD?

It's located at Holliday Park in Cheyenne. "Big Boy" was the largest steam locomotive ever built. Conceived by the mechanical department of the Union Pacific, Number 4004 was built in 1941 by the American Locomotive Company.

Altogether, twenty-four "Big Boys" worked over the rugged country between Cheyenne, Wyoming and Ogden, Utah. One of the Union Pacific engineers said about the giant steam locomotives:

> If one of those bulls won't go over
> the mountain, it'll go through it!

With the passing of the steam locomotive, Number 4004 was retired in 1956. In 1963 it was donated to the city of Cheyenne by the Union Pacific Railroad and placed in Holliday Park.

The following are "Big Boy" specifications:

Total weight: 1,208,750 lbs.
Overall length: 132 ft. 9 in.
Coal capacity: 28 tons
Water capacity: 25,000 gallons
Driving wheel diameter: 68 in.
Firebox: 96 in. × 235 in.
Fuel: soft coal
Total evaporating surface: 5,889 sq. ft.
Maximum tractive power: 135,375 lbs.

WHERE IS ONE OF THE MOST FAMOUS MUSEUMS OF THE AMERICAN WEST?

In the town of Cody, founded by William F. Cody in 1897, is the outstanding Buffalo Bill Historical Center. The facility contains not only the Buffalo Bill Museum, but the Plains Indians Museum, the Whitney Gallery of Western Art, Winchester Museum as well as Cody's boyhood home. The gray clapboard house was moved to the grounds from LeClair, Iowa. Cody, one of the best known characters in the West, was born in LeClaire on February 26, 1846. He died in Denver on January 10, 1917, and was buried in Colorado.

WHAT WYOMING TOWN WAS THE HOME OF THE WORLD'S LARGEST WINDMILL?

Medicine Bow in Carbon County in the southeastern part of the state had the world's largest windmill. It was built at a site five miles south of the town, and was dedicated in September 1982.

Two giant wind turbines were constructed for the U.S. Department of the Interior's Bureau of Reclamation. They were erected to determine the feasibility of using modern wind turbines to generate electrical power. Together, the two turbines could have had the capacity of generating 6.5 megawatts of electricity per year, enough for 3,000 homes. Even though the tall wind turbines had been expected to save 20,000 barrels of oil a year the project was abandoned in the late 1980s.

WHO IS CONSIDERED THE "ELDER" OF GRAND TETON MOUNTAIN CLIMBERS?

Paul Petzoldt, founder of the National Outdoor Leadership School in Lander, in July, 1984, completed his 60th anniversary ascent of the Grand Teton Range of Western Wyoming.

This internationally-known mountain climber was accompanied by a party of twenty-five, many of whom made the fiftieth anniversary ascent with Petzoldt in 1974. One member of the party claims that Petzoldt is now the undisputed elder of Grand Teton climbers.

"He's the oldest gentleman to climb the Grand Teton," Mike Zeno said, adding that climbs of the Grand Teton Range are well documented.

The book, *On Top of the World*, by Patricia McGarity Petzoldt, formerly of Riverton, describes Paul Petzoldt's mountain climbing adventures in many parts of the world.

WHERE ARE COLLECTIONS OF INDIAN ARTIFACTS AND CULTURAL MATERIALS?

The Buffalo Bill Historical Center in Cody has the outstanding Plains Indians Museum. St. Michaels Mission at Ethete in Fremont County has beaded and porcupine quill work. The Museum at Colter Bay has a rare display. The State Museum in Cheyenne has an Indian collection and many town and city museums display Indian crafts and artifacts.

WHAT IS THE LARGEST SINGLE REVENUE SOURCE FOR THE STATE OF WYOMING?

Oil makes up 40 percent of Wyoming's $7.9 billion assessed valuation. According to the state Department of Revenue and Taxation, crude oil production in Wyoming was valued at $3.2 billion in 1983, more than coal and natural gas valuations combined.

In the article, "Oil: State's Largest Revenue Producer," appearing in the *Riverton Ranger* on June 19, 1984, Publisher, Robert A. Peck, wrote:

> Oil produced more than 50 percent of Wyoming's total mineral taxes in 1983, estimated at nearly $124 mil-

lion dollars... Oil and gas property
account for 57 percent of the state's
total assessed valuation... Wyoming
has the sixth largest proven oil and
gas reserves in the nation.

WHAT IS THE LARGEST HIGH-ALTITUDE LAKE IN NORTH AMERICA?

Yellowstone Lake, with an altitude of 7,331 feet, is
in Yellowstone National Park. This natural fresh-water lake, with a total area of 139 square miles, is
popular with fishermen from all over the United
States. There are many geysers on the bottom of
this beautiful body of water.

WHERE'S THE WORLD'S LARGEST BAR MADE OF JADE?

The forty-foot jade bar is in the town of Medicine
Bow at the Diplodocus Bar. The green jade was cut
from a huge boulder near Rock Springs. The tavern
also displays trophy mounts from the Medicine Bow
area.
Jade became the official stone of Wyoming Janu-ary 25, 1967. It is found along the Sweetwater River
and in the sagebrush prairies of Fremont and
Sweetwater counties.

WHERE IS ONE OF THE WORLD'S LARGEST WILDLIFE SANCTUARIES?

More than 200 species of birds now inhabit Yel-lowstone National Park, including the yellow-headed blackbird. Bears, mountain sheep, elk, deer,
bison, moose and hundreds of smaller animals live in
the area that includes thousands of acres. One small
mammal which intrigues tourists is the smokey-gray Townsend squirrel, often called a picket pin. It
lives in the sagebrush and grassland.

Why are they called picket pins? Because they stand like sentries at the entrances to their burrows.

At the Norris Trailside Museum are displays of birds mounted in colored dioramas. Some of the birds that build their nests in the park are the mountain bluebird, finch, crossbill, flycatcher, bunting, white-crowned sparrow, desert sparrow hawk, red-shafted flicker, mountain chickadee, gray ruffed grouse, western tanager, and killdeer.

A natural wonder that intrigues visitors at Mammoth are the hot springs. Jupiter Terrace is said to be the largest travertine terrace in the world. Algae which thrive on the hot and tepid waters, cover it with rich colors.

Another unusual wonder in this two-million-plus acre park is Obsidian Cliff. This mountainside of volcanic glass, black as anthracite, is covered by lichens and mosses. Years ago Indian people used the glassy material for arrowheads and spearheads, as well as for skinning knives.

FROM UNEXPLORED WILDERNESS UNTIL 1869

WHICH INDIAN TRIBES ONCE HUNTED IN WILDERNESS WYOMING?

Twelve tribes hunted in wilderness Wyoming. They were the Arapaho, Bannock, Blackfeet, Cheyenne, Crow, Flathead, Kiowa, Modoc, Nez Perce, Shoshone, Sioux and Ute.

An abstract design of the first people in wilderness Wyoming.

IS THERE AN INDIAN
RESERVATION IN WYOMING?

The Shoshone Reservation, now called the Wind River Reservation, was created by the federal government at the Fort Bridger Council in 1868. The first reservation to be established in wilderness Wyoming, it's still the only Indian reserve in the state.

Chief Washakie and seven Shoshone men as well as Chief Targhee and several Bannock Indians placed their x's on the document. Seven military men, representing the United States government, also signed.

The Bannock Indians left shortly for Fort Hall in wilderness Idaho, to be with their own people. The Bannocks never lived on the two million-plus-acre Wind River Reservation.

WHERE CAN YOU SEE IRON
BEDSTEADS IN A CEMETERY?

There are many old iron bedsteads at the Sacajawea Cemetery on the Wind River Reservation in Fremont County, a few miles from Fort Washakie.

The Shoshone people believe that when a member of their tribe is buried, the deceased should take all personal belongings. Bags, suitcases, Stetson hats, shawls, blankets and other personal belongings are piled on top of the casket, but beaded articles and deer skin clothing are placed inside with the body.

In early days Shoshone people placed the deceased's iron bedstead on top of the mound, using it as a marker. In the Sacajawea Cemetery there are many iron bedsteads, now painted white, on the graves of Shoshone men and women who died many years ago. However, the custom of using bedsteads as markers was discontinued long ago.

22

Long ago Shoshone Indians planted iron bedsteads on earthen mounds, using them as markers. A number of them, now painted white, are in the Sacajawea Cemetery at Fort Washakie in Fremont County, near the Wind River Mountains.

WHO WERE THE FIRST WHITE MEN TO EXPLORE THE UNKNOWN WILDERNESS?

They were French Canadian explorers who were in search of the Western sea. In 1742, the year George Washington was ten years old, two brothers, Francois and Louis Joseph Verendrye, with two fellow Frenchmen, began an important, historic journey. After leaving the Mandan Indian villages in present-day North Dakota, they traveled westward, possibly as far as the high mountains now called the Big Horns near the present city of Sheridan. But they abandoned their search for the Western ocean because of hostility they encountered from the Shoshone Indians.

In the area where Pierre, the capital of South Dakota, is now located, school children discovered, in 1913, the lead plate that had been buried on the east bank of the Missouri River by the French Canadian explorers on their return trip.

WHO WERE THE FIRST WHITE MEN TO USE SOUTH PASS?

Robert Stuart, the American explorer who was born in Scotland, joined the John Jacob Astor venture on the West Coast, and in 1812 led a party of "Astorians" east. He and his rugged men were the first known to have used the South Pass and to have followed the main route that later became the famous Oregon Trail.

DID THE LEWIS AND CLARK EXPEDITION GO THROUGH THE WYOMING AREA?

No, Lewis and Clark did not travel as far south as Wyoming. During the most significant 4,000 mile transcontinental journey made from 1804-1806, Meriwether Lewis and his army friend William Clark served as leaders of the expedition. Among those who accompanied them were the dog, Shannon, and a Negro man named York.

The expedition reached the foothills of the Rocky Mountains in June 1805, in what is now southwestern Montana. Later, Sacajawea, a young Shoshone woman and wife of the guide Charbonneau, served as interpreter with members of her tribe. The Shoshones supplied horses and squaws to serve as baggage carriers over the Continental Divide at Lemhi Pass, Idaho.

WHO WAS THE FIRST WHITE SETTLER IN WYOMING?

Edward Rose, a member of the trapping party led by Ezekel Williams who came into the area in 1807, was the first white settler in the Big Horn Basin. Ezekel Williams and the other men in his party are often referred to as the "lost trappers," because of reports of their wanderings.

WHAT'S A RENDEZVOUS?

A rendezvous is a pre-arranged meeting place, bringing people together at a specified time. The word *rendezvous* comes from the French verb rendez-vous, meaning "render yourselves" or "repair to a place."

From 1825 through 1840, American, English and French fur trappers, tradesmen from the eastern states and Indian hunters traveled long distances to attend the annual summer trade fairs in the Rocky Mountains. They were held in meadowland along the rivers so there would be wild grass to feed the horses and mules.

During the rendezvous, mountain men sold or traded beaver skins for much needed supplies and celebrated with friends and rivals.

Jesuit priest Father Pierre Jean De Smet attended the last rendezvous held on the Green River in 1840. He recorded the celebration in *Life, Letters and Travels of Father De Smet 1801-1872:*

> The rendezvous was one of the most
> interesting developments of the fur
> trade in the Rocky Mountains...
> These meetings were great events
> and form one of the most pictur-
> esque features of early frontier life
> in the Far West.

Twelve of the sixteen summer trade fairs, called rendezvous, were held in the wilderness later known as Wyoming, in the valleys of the Green, Wind and Popo Agie rivers.

WHICH EXPLORER BLAZED A TRAIL FROM ST. LOUIS TO THE PACIFIC COAST?

Wilson Price Hunt and his party crossed the northern boundary into the area now known as Wyoming about August 1, 1811. Then, with his company of men known as the Astorians, Hunt traveled to the West, leaving by way of the canyon he had named for trapper-guide, John Hoback. They traveled through the somewhat narrow opening in the Teton Range now called Teton Pass.

Hunt's journey was important for it followed a route through wilderness never before taken by white men. In 340 days, Hunt and his men blazed the way across the continent from St. Louis to the Pacific Coast. By mapping out a central land route from the Missouri River to the Oregon wilderness, the vast expanse of prairie and mountains now known as Wyoming was thus brought into American history.

WHO NAMED INDEPENDENCE ROCK THE "REGISTER OF THE DESERT?"

In 1840, Father Pierre Jean DeSmet, first Jesuit priest to travel through the Rocky Mountains, called the granite monolith the "Register of the Desert" because emigrants scratched their names on the hard stone. The unusual grayish-brown rock, almost 2,000 feet long and about 167 feet high, is on the north side of the Sweetwater River in present-day Natrona County. Many of the 50,000 names have been weathered by the rain and wind, but there are thousands that still remain readable.

The first meeting of the Masonic (A. F. & A. M.) Lodge, held on July 4, 1862 in the area now called Wyoming, was at Independence Rock. A few miles south are Devil's Gate and Split Rock, both landmarks for the men, women and children heading westward.

WHEN DID THE AMERICAN FLAG FIRST FLY OVER THE WIND RIVER MOUNTAINS?

Captain John C. Fremont unfurled the American flag on August 14, 1842. Thinking that he was on the highest peak in the Wind River Range, he planted the flag with twenty-six stars in a field of blue, and the thirteen red and white stripes. Fremont was mistaken, however, for Gannett Peak is the highest peak with an altitude of 13,785 feet.

Orrin H. Bonney and Lorraine Bonney, in their well-researched book, *Guide to the Wyoming Mountains and the Wilderness Areas*, claim that Fremont climbed Mt. Woodrow Wilson (13,500 feet plus). This peak is about one mile south of Gannett Peak on the Continental Divide in the southwest corner of the Dinwoody Glacier cirque. Climbing with Fremont were Charles Preuss, the artist Basil Lejeuness, Clement Lambert, Johnie Janisse and deCoteau.

The next ascent was eighty-two years later, on September 2, 1924, when Dr. Carol Jones, the Reverend Albert Bessie and Dr. Edgar A. Doll climbed the peak via Route I. The party named it Woodrow Wilson Peak because it appeared to have fourteen points. Following World War I, President Woodrow Wilson had proposed fourteen points as guidelines for the first major world peace organization, the League of Nations, which was dedicated to international cooperation and the prevention of war.

WHEN WAS THE FIRST FOURTH OF JULY CELEBRATION AT INDEPENDENCE ROCK?

The huge turtle-shaped monolith located on the north bank of the Sweetwater River was known as the "Register of the Desert" before 1847. On the nation's seventy-first birthday, weary-worn travelers who were bound for the West, assembled near the huge granite rock to celebrate the Fourth of July. Having no firecrackers, the men lighted sticks of dynamite. Many names were inscribed on the rock that Sunday, July 4, 1847. Since that time the famous monolith has been known as Independence Rock.

HOW LONG WAS THE OREGON TRAIL?

The Oregon Trail, used by emigrants for more than 2,000 miles beyond the frontier, extended from Independence, Missouri to the Columbia River.

The main trail followed the Platte River to Fort Laramie in Wyoming, passing through the Wind River Mountains of the Central Rockies by way of South Pass. It then ran along the Snake River and crossed the Blue Mountains into the Willamette Valley of Oregon.

More than 300,000 men, women and children traveled across wilderness Wyoming from 1840 until 1869.

WHO MADE THE LONGEST PONY EXPRESS RIDE ON RECORD?

Fifteen-year-old William F. Cody, born in Iowa, made the hectic ride in 1860. Called Will in his younger years, he was later known as "Buffalo Bill" Cody due to his expertise in shooting buffalo that roamed the plains.

Will Cody mounted his horse, with the mail bags already securely strapped, and started from Red Butte on the Platte River to Three Crossings, seventy-six miles away. When he arrived he was told that his replacement rider had been killed, so without resting, he rode the eighty-five mile stretch to Rocky Ridge. He then made the return trip to Red Butte within the scheduled time.

The 322-mile trip is the longest on record for the Pony Express.

HOW MANY PONY EXPRESS
STATIONS WERE IN THIS STATE?

According to Dr. T. A. Larson, author of the book, *History of Wyoming*, there were forty Pony Express stations, eight to twenty miles apart, along the southern part of Wyoming's wilderness. The stations included:

Fort Laramie
Horse Shoe
Bed Tick
Deer Creek
Red Butte
Sweetwater
Split Rock
Three Crossings
Big Sandy
Fort Bridger

WHEN DID THE PONY EXPRESS
CROSS WILDERNESS WYOMING?

Although the Pony Express was in operation only eighteen months, it was an important form of communication before the advent of the telegraph. It began in 1860 when riders of the Pony Express crossed the mountains and plains on the emigrant trails in wilderness Wyoming. The riders carried mail from St. Joseph, Missouri, to Sacramento, California, and back.

HOW MANY BUFFALO ONCE
GRAZED ON THE GREAT PLAINS?

In the early decades of the 19th century, as many as 60 million American bison, commonly called buffalo, still trampled the Great Plains. Peter Matthiessen in his book *Wildlife in America*, stated that bison often "turned the prairies to seas of black." He claims that the bison herds were "the greatest animal congregations that ever existed on the earth."

In his early years, William Frederick Cody, better known as "Buffalo Bill" Cody, worked as a hunter. He stated:

> I killed buffalo for the railroad company (the Union Pacific) for twelve months, and during that time the number I brought into camp were kept account of, and at the end of that period I had killed 4,280 buffalo...

By the end of 1883, with the exception of stray buffalo, these large hoofed mammals were gone from North America. The herds were wiped out by hunters, climatic changes and overgrazing by cattle.

HOW MANY EMIGRANTS TRAVELED ACROSS WYOMING FROM 1840 TO 1860?

There may have been as many as 300,000 men, women and children who traveled in covered wagons, on horseback, by mule or on foot, some even pushing hand carts across the prairie and over the hills.

WHAT ARE THE HISTORICAL TRAILS AND ROADS IN WYOMING?

They are the:

Mormon Trail
California Trail
Oregon Trail
Sublette Cut Off
Overland Stage Route
Original Pony Express
Bozeman Trail

Lander Cut Off
Bridger Trail
Cheyenne-Deadwood Stage Road
Black Hills Wagon Road
Wilson Price Hunt Trail
Robert Stuart Trail
Captain Bonneville Trail
Overland or Cherokee Trail
Texas Trail.

WHEN WAS THE TELEGRAPH LINE COMPLETED IN WYOMING?

The federal government offered a subsidy of $40,000 a year for ten years to the builder of the first telegraph line across the plains. Edward Creighton, the successful competitor, completed the Overland transcontinental telegraph line across wilderness Wyoming along the old emigrant trail in 1861. The Indians called the telegraph lines the "talking wires."

WHEN WAS THE BLOODY YEAR ON THE PLAINS?

The year was 1867. There had been trouble with Indian tribes the preceding decade, but there were many more attacks between 1862 and 1868.

In 1867, Indian warriors and braves constantly attacked the emigrant wagon trains and stage stations as well as the Platte Bridge site where, in July, 1865, Lieutenant Caspar Collins was killed.

General P. E. Connor came to this area in 1863 to protect the Overland Stage Route from Fort Kearney, Nebraska, to Salt Lake City, Utah.

During the 1860s the U.S. government built a number of outposts, including Fort Sanders in 1866, a few miles from Fort Laramie; Fort Fetterman on the Platte River near Douglas, and Fort D. A. Russell, later renamed Fort Francis E. Warren, on Crow Creek.

WHAT IS THE CROWHEART BUTTE STORY?

One of the most striking landmarks, east of the Wind River Range in Fremont County, is the large flat-top hill with sloping sides that rises high above sagebrush plains and alfalfa fields. Crowheart Butte can be seen for miles along highway 26-287 between Kinnear and almost to the red rocks near Dubois.

Some years before the Shoshones in 1868 were given their reservation, including Crowheart Butte, many battles were fought among a number of Indian tribes for control of the extensive hunting grounds in the Wind River Basin.

One spring day the Shoshones, with Chief Washakie, were hunting for big game in the upper country near present-day Kinnear, an area the Shoshones considered their domain. When they saw Crow Indians chasing herds of buffalo across their hunting grounds, Chief Washakie sent a young brave and his wife to the enemy camp to warn the Crow hunters to leave the Shoshones' Warm Valley at once.

The enemies were furious. They killed the young brave, but his wife escaped. Washakie then sent word to his allies, Chief Targhee and the Bannocks, who soon joined the Shoshone warriors. A long battle ensued since both tribes were evenly matched.

Legend says that on the last day, whether by chance or agreement, two angry chiefs, Washakie and Big Robber, met in personal combat on top of the high flat mound. They raced toward each other on their war ponies, their spears, long shafts with sharply pointed heads, in position ready for action. When the powerful warriors met on impact, both chiefs fell from their horses. The fateful fight then continued on foot with Washakie the victor.

The winner cut out the Crow chief's heart and displayed it on his spear. Stories vary about whether Chief Washakie actually ate his enemy's heart.

One Wyoming historian wrote that when asked about the event, Washakie, then an old man, is reported to have said:

> When a man is in battle and his
> blood runs hot, he sometimes does
> things that he is sorry afterwards. I
> cannot remember everything that
> happened so long ago.

WAS FORT CASPAR A MAJOR OUTPOST?

Fort Caspar was a major fort in 1867, prior to the building of Fort Fetterman near Douglas on the North Platte River. About 450 to 500 soldiers were stationed at the military outpost during the summer of 1867.

The informative sign at the Fort Caspar Museum in the town of Casper reads:

> Originally known to trappers and
> explorers (1830-1847) as Upper
> Crossing of the North Platte River, it
> became the Mormon Ferry in 1847.
> Guinard built a bridge here in 1858,
> and troops from Platte River Station
> guarded the telegraph line and pro-
> tected emigrants on the Oregon
> Trail. July 26, 1865, the station was
> attacked by hordes of Indians. Lt.
> Caspar Collins led an heroic attempt
> to rescue Sgt. Custard's wagon train,
> but sacrificed his life in aiding a
> fallen soldier. The station was
> renamed Fort Caspar in his honor.
> Abandoned in 1867, fort and bridge
> were burned by the Indians. The old
> fort was restored on its original
> foundations in 1936.

The museum is now located on the site of the old calvary fort.

Casper, one of Wyoming's largest cities, was named for the brave officer, but the city's name is spelled with an *e*, not an *a*. Lt. Caspar Collins spelled his given name with an *a*.

WHO INTRODUCED THE BILL TO CREATE THE TERRITORY OF WYOMING?

James M. Ashley, congressman from Ohio, on January 5, 1865 introduced a bill before the thirty-eighth Congress to create the Territory of Wyoming. It died, however, in committee. Ashley had suggested the name "Wyoming" for the Western land, and it alone survived the bill's defeat.

Three years later, on February 13, 1868, Richard Yates, an Illinois senator, introduced a bill before the forty-fourth Congress. This time it received the necessary number of votes.

WHEN WAS WYOMING TERRITORY OFFICIALLY ORGANIZED?

The Organic Act of Wyoming, approved July 25, 1868, created Wyoming Territory from sections of Dakota, Utah and Idaho. However, the Territory could not organize until after the executive and judicial officers were appointed and qualified. The Fortieth Congress, third session, failed to confirm the executive and judicial appointments President Andrew Johnson had made for Wyoming Territory. No doubt this was due to the feud between Congress and the President over Johnson's impeachment. Because of this delay, Wyoming Territory was not officially organized until May 19, 1869.

President Ulysses S. Grant, who followed Johnson as U.S. chief executive, appointed John A. Campbell Wyoming's first territorial governor. Campbell had been U.S. Assistant Secretary of War.

Cheyenne was designated the territorial capital on May 25, 1869. The first census recorded 8,014 people. At that time there were four counties: Albany, Carbon, Carter and Laramie. Each county extended from the northern border to the southern border.

Phatty Thompson earned a small fortune by selling Cheyenne cats in Deadwood City. But enroute to sell his cargo, his wagon upset, spilling cats in every direction.

FROM TERRITORIAL DAYS TO STATEHOOD AND INTO THE 20th CENTURY

HAVE CATS EVER PLAYED A ROLE IN WYOMING'S HISTORY?

One of the most unusual shipments ever hauled over the stage route between Cheyenne and Deadwood City was in 1877. "Phatty" Thompson, an independent freighter who owned a wagon and mules, decided one day that the girls at dance halls in Deadwood City needed pets. So he offered twenty-five cents for every stray cat Cheyenne boys could find in alleys, around butcher shops and other stores.

After the teamster had loaded the crate of howling cats at the Elephant Corral in Cheyenne, he headed north to the Dakotas. But Phatty met with disaster along the way. Enroute to Deadwood the wagon tipped over, upsetting the crate, with frightened felines running in every direction. The freighter did not give up, however. He succeeded in catching most of the hungry cats with food, probably enticing them with chunks of meat.

So once again he headed north. When he arrived in Deadwood City, Phatty Thompson was well rewarded. He sold the cats at exorbitant prices, many for $10 per feline. Some of the girls paid as high as $25 for their new pets.

WHERE WAS THE INFAMOUS CHINESE MASSACRE IN 1885?

The Chinese massacre in 1885 was in Rock Springs. Only white men worked in the Union Pacific coal mines prior to 1875. Later, when the miners went on strike, Chinese laborers were hired as strikebreakers. Less than two weeks after the white miners struck, company officials fired the men. Work at the coal mines was resumed, however, with fifty white miners and 150 Chinese miners.

On September 2, 1885, tragedy struck the coal mining town. In the anti-Chinese riot, twenty-eight Chinese were killed. Fifteen others were wounded and several hundred Chinese were chased out of town. Rioters destroyed property valued at more than $147,000. Racial prejudice had been smoldering for years. Also there was bitterness against the officials of the Union Pacific Coal Department.

The following day Territorial Governor Francis E. Warren personally investigated the outburst and immediately sent a telegram to President Grover Cleveland, requesting troops. A week later soldiers escorted the Chinese people back to Rock Springs. The U.S. Congress, later that same year, voted to pay the Chinese $147,748.74 for their losses, on the recommendation of President Cleveland.

WHAT YEAR DID GOVERNOR WARREN SIGN THE BILL AUTHORIZING THE BUILDING OF THE CAPITOL?

In his message to the Ninth Legislative Assembly in 1886, Territorial Governor Francis E. Warren spoke of the need for public buildings. The Legislature agreed and passed a bill authorizing the construction of a Capitol with the cost not to exceed $150,000. Governor Warren signed the bill. The five men appointed to the Capitol Building Commission then began the selection of a site and design. The site the Commission chose cost $13,000. That area is now known as Capitol Avenue. Later the Commission decided on the style:

> The front (of the Capitol) to be treated on the French Renaissance class of architecture; the rear to correspond, but not to be treated so expensively.

The *Cheyenne Daily* reported that the laying of the Capitol cornerstone on May 18, 1887 was "the occasion of the greatest military and civic demonstration ever witnessed in the history of the city." Territorial and city officials, United States troops from Fort D.A. Russell, bands, firemen, bicyclists, members of different societies, the Grand Lodge A.F & A.M. of Wyoming and other Masonic bodies marched through the streets of Cheyenne, past buildings decorated with flags and banners. The parade ended at the partially finished Capitol.

Wyoming's Capitol, the book The Wyoming State Press published in 1987, describes the laying of the cornerstone by N.R. Davis, Grand Master, and members of the Grand Lodge A.F. & A.M.:

> As the crowd gathered, the Masons took their positions on a temporary platform built at the cornerstone to the left of the Capitol entrance. The cornerstone, a fine piece of Rawlins sandstone, hung suspended by a derrick. Scooped out of its under surface was sufficient space to admit a copper box sixteen inches in length, twelve inches wide and seven inches deep. In it were placed items such as the laws of Wyoming, an impression of the great seal of the territory, various territorial newspapers, timetables of the

Union Pacific Railroad and several photographs...

After the cornerstone was in place, the crowd gathered just west of the unfinished Capitol building. Several thousand people enjoyed the barbecue which consisted of pork, mutton, bread, "cornerstone pickles," lemonade and roast beef.

WHO GAVE WYOMING THE POPULAR NICKNAME OF "EQUALITY STATE?"

Robert C. Morris, Territorial Historian, gave Wyoming the popular nickname of "The Equality State." Morris, one of the members of the House of Representatives from Sweetwater County in 1907 and 1909, was the son of Esther Hobart Morris of South Pass City, who, in 1870, was the first woman justice of the peace in the United States.

The Wyoming historian stated that the reason for suggesting "The Equality State," was that the Constitution provided that "The Rights of the Citizens of the State of Wyoming to vote and hold office shall not be denied or abridged on account of sex. Both Male and Female Citizens of this State shall equally enjoy all civil, political and religious rights and privileges."

The great seal of Wyoming bears upon its face the motto of "Equal Rights" while the corporate seal of the State University has for its motto "Equality."

WHAT DAM WAS WYOMING'S FIRST FEDERAL PROJECT?

The Buffalo Bill Dam was Wyoming's first federal project. It has been designated as a National Historic Civil Engineering Landmark, the only one in the state.

Lessons learned from engineering problems solved in construction of the Shoshone Dam, now known as the Buffalo Bill Dam, have been applied to other important reservoir projects in various parts of the United States.

The original name "Shoshone" was changed to the Buffalo Bill Dam by a Congressional act to honor the world-famous showman, Col. William F. Cody, better known as "Buffalo Bill." His home was in Cody, Wyoming, the town named for him.

Cody and Nate Salesbury started the project in 1899, expecting the reservoir would mean the reclaiming of thousands of acres of arid land. But the two men ran out of funds, and were ready to relinquish their water rights; however, the state later issued the rights to the federal government.

The 325-foot-high dam, built across the Shoshone River, was completed in 1910.

WHEN WAS THE BUCKING HORSE PUT ON WYOMING LICENSE PLATES?

In 1936 the picture of the cowboy on the bucking bronco was drawn by Allen T. True of Denver. His brother James B. True was, at the time, Wyoming's state highway engineer.

Many people have claimed that the rider was "Stub" Farlow of Lander, and the horse was the famous Steamboat. Lester C. Hunt, governor of Wyoming, and later a U.S. Senator, said he had Stub Farlow in mind when the plate was designed, but the cowboy from Fremont County was not the model for the license plate, which is still considered one of the most distinctive and striking of all automobile plates.

WHAT IMPORTANT CASE WAS DECIDED IN FAVOR OF THE SHOSHONE INDIANS?

The U.S. Congress passed the act (Statute 1349) on March 3, 1927, which enabled the Shoshones to sue in Court of Claims for that portion of the Indian reservation occupied by the Arapahos since 1878.

The Shoshone people, who sued the U.S. government, claimed that the Arapahos had occupied their reserve, now called the Wind River Reservation, for sixty years without reimbursement to them.

Volume II of the *Wyoming Blue Book* reported:

> A final judgment of $6,364,377, less offsets, is reached (in 1938) in the Shoshone case against the government... After the cost of the suit and the government's non-treaty expenditures are deducted, the balance paid to the Shoshones is about four million dollars. The case clears title to the lands which the Arapahos have occupied on a temporary basis since 1878, and the Arapahos become co-owners of the Wind River Reservation.

WHAT ARE WYOMING'S EMBLEMS?

The state emblems are:

Flag: adopted in 1917
Flower: Indian paintbrush, 1917
Seal: (the great seal), 1921
Bird: meadowlark, 1927
Tree: cottonwood, 1947
Motto: "Equal Rights," 1955
Song: "Wyoming," 1955
Gemstone: jade, 1967

The cottonwood tree, the prototype of the Wyoming State Tree, was the largest of its kind in the United States. This tall tree *(Populus sargentii)* stood on the Paul Klein ranch a few miles north of Thermopolis in Hot Springs County. Originally the land was homesteaded by J. M. Cover. Possibly three or four hundred years old, the cottonwood tree measured 29 feet in circumference and 76 feet 11 inches in height. For years Wyoming residents and tourists, driving north on the highway towards Worland, admired this lone tree growing on the farm. Unfortunately the cottonwood tree burned down in 1955. The farmer who was burning weeds nearby could not save the tree when the fire got out of control.

The author's father, George F. Dobler, a lawyer and judge in Fremont County, was chairman of the Judiciary Committee for the House of Representatives in 1917 when the state flag, designed with the bison, and the state flower, the Indian paintbrush, were officially adopted.

WHO WAS THE FIRST WYOMING INDIAN CONVICTED IN A WHITE MAN'S COURT?

Yellow Eagle, a respected member of the Northern Arapaho Tribe, who raised horses in the eastern section of the Shoshone Reservation, was accused of horse stealing. A white man, Louis Peterson, who ranched on the reservation, had accused the Arapaho of stealing three of his horses.

Yellow Eagle was arrested Thursday, July 12, 1887, and taken to jail in Lander. A few days later the trial was held in the Fremont County Courthouse, where the Arapaho man was found guilty and sentenced to prison.

There were many ranchers in the county who were indignant about the sentence. More than fifty prominent ranchers and county citizens signed a petition for Yellow Eagle's release, and Colonel

Thomas M. Jones, Indian agent at Fort Washakie, interceded on the Arapaho man's behalf.

Thomas Moonlight, governor of Wyoming Territory, granted a pardon to Yellow Eagle two months later on September 13, 1887.

WHO WAS THE ONLY GOVERNOR OF WYOMING BORN IN A FOREIGN COUNTRY?

Thomas Moonlight was territorial governor of Wyoming from January 24, 1887 to April 9, 1889. President Grover Cleveland made the appointment. Moonlight, a Democrat, was born in Forfarshire, Scotland. He came to America at the age of thirteen.

His proclamation in 1889 made Arbor Day a legal holiday in the Territory of Wyoming, and reveals Moonlight's Scottish-American philosophy:

> It is said that a certain man when dying, called his son and heir to his bedside and gave him his last request, "Aye be planting trees, they'll grow when you're asleep."

WHAT'S THE MOST POPULAR COMMUNITY SPORT IN WYOMING?

Rodeo. No holiday, such as the fourth of July or Labor Day, or an anniversary of a town could be celebrated in Wyoming without cowboys and bucking animals. Certainly the crowds would be disappointed if there wasn't a rodeo at every county fair.

Rodeo performers are not only young men and women. At the Old Timers' Rodeo, men, who in former years have won loving cups, belt buckles and cash awards, perform with enthusiasm as well as a certain amount of expertise. Men and women in the grandstand hail them as heroes even though the bucking horses and bulls are the winners.

Of course the "Daddy of 'Em All" is the Frontier Days celebration that draws people from all over the U.S. and foreign countries. By far the most popular event is the cowboy, rigged in Western gear, precariously seated astride a bucking bronco.

One of the most popular events at Frontier Days is the bucking bronco. The celebration is held in Cheyenne in late July. The state's first commercial rodeo was held in Lander in Fremont County in 1893.

WERE CATTLEMEN RESPONSIBLE FOR THE ONLY WOMAN EVER HANGED, LEGALLY OR ILLEGALLY, IN WYOMING?

Ella Mae Watson, better known as "Cattle Kate," is the only woman ever lynched in Wyoming. On July 20, 1889, James Averell, a well-educated Easterner whose homestead was on land in Carbon County where A. J. Bothwell formerly grazed his stock, and Watson, who ran cattle on her homestead, were hanged as rustlers. The lynching took place on the Sweetwater River, not far from Independence Rock.

In the late 19th century, rustling on the open range was a serious problem. Stockmen also were at war with the nesters who were settling on land in cattle-grazing country. Averell had written letters to the Casper *Daily Mail* complaining that three men were attempting to take over several hundred miles of prime grassland along the Sweetwater River. Stockmen were suspicious, claiming cowboys had given Cattle Kate stolen cattle in return for her favors. Ranchers not only branded Cattle Kate and Averell as troublemakers, but also accused her of rustling.

On that fateful Sunday in 1889 less than a year before Wyoming was admitted as the 44th state in the Union, Cattle Kate and James Averell were hanged.

The article, "A Double Lynching," printed in the Cheyenne *Daily Leader* on Tuesday, July 23, 1889, stated:

> Ropes were hung from the limb of a
> big cottonwood tree on the south
> bank of the Sweetwater. Nooses
> were adjusted to the necks of Averill
> (sic) and his wife and their horses led
> from under them. The woman died
> with curses on her foul lips...

In his book *History of Wyoming*, Dr. T. A. Larson wrote that the coroner's jury reported that Averell and Ella Mae Watson "came to their deaths by being hanged by the neck at the hands of A. J. Bothwell, Tom Sun, John Durbin, R. M. Galbraith, Bob Connor, E. McIain and an unknown man."

Jean Mead in *Casper Country* (1987) wrote that George Henderson, who reportedly hanged Ella Watson, was never arrested nor was he mentioned in the trial. However, Frank Hadsell, Carbon County sheriff, arrested the other men. Later they were released under "five thousand dollars bond." There is no record of the cattlemen ever being punished for the double lynching. Averell's horse was sold later at a sheriff's sale. It is still a mystery about what happened to Averell and Watson's cattle. Mari Sandoz, author of *The Cattlemen*, wrote that Henry H. Wilson contested the two homesteads on the ground of desertion. When the final proof was recorded, Wilson sold the land to Bothwell.

Newspapers throughout the United States condemned "the barbaric lynching of a woman in Wyoming Territory."

HOW MANY PREHISTORIC SITES HAVE BEEN DISCOVERED IN WYOMING?

According to a July 16, 1984 article in the *Casper Star-Tribune*, more than 35,000 sites, both historic and prehistoric, have been discovered in Wyoming, although ninety-seven percent of the state has yet to be surveyed.

The remains of extinct mammoths, camels, bison, horses and other mammals, have been found by professional archeologists as well as by amateur enthusiasts, according to George Frison, former Wyoming State archeologist.

The Wyoming Historic Preservation Office exercises authority to protect sites only by federal law.

WHAT PRESIDENT'S FATHER AND GRANDFATHER WERE WYOMINGITES?

Gerald Ford's father, Leslie L. King, and his paternal grandfather C. H. King, one of the state's earliest entrepreneurs and wealthiest men during the early 1900s, lived for many years in Wyoming.

Ford's father and mother were staying in the elegant C. H. King home in Omaha in July 1913 when their son Leslie L. King, Jr. was born. Several months later they were divorced. His mother Dorothy King and stepfather Gerald Ford, Sr. were married in Grand Rapids, Michigan, and the young boy was then known as Gerry Ford to his schoolmates and friends. He changed his name legally to Gerald Ford, Jr. shortly after his twenty-first birthday.

Gerald Ford's paternal grandfather first established a store in Douglas, and later with his family moved to Casper, where he was successful in transportation projects as well as the sheep industry. It is said that C. H. King was instrumental in getting the Chicago and North Western Railroad to extend its line in 1906 from Shoshoni to Lander in Fremont County.

For years Leslie L. King was an officer in the lumber company in Riverton.

FOR HOW MANY YEARS WAS WYOMING A TERRITORY?

Twenty-two years. Wyoming was admitted as the forty-fourth state on July 10, 1890, seven days after Idaho attained statehood.

WHO WAS THE FIRST GRADUATE OF THE UNIVERSITY OF WYOMING TO BECOME GOVERNOR?

Milward L. Simpson, who served as Wyoming's chief executive from 1955 to 1959, was the first graduate of Wyoming's only university to become governor. Born in Jackson in 1897, Simpson was reared on the Wind River Reservation, in Lander, Meeteetse, and Cody. His maternal grandfather Finn Burnett came to Wyoming in 1865 with the Powder River Expedition led by General Patrick E. Connor. Later Burnett worked as the head farmer on the reservation. Milward's paternal grandfather

John Simpson came to Wyoming in 1884. He opened the first store and post office in the Jackson Hole area.

Milward Simpson's father W. I. Simpson was an attorney in Wyoming for fifty years. His mother Margaret Simpson, born January 24, 1874, celebrated her 100th birthday in 1974 at Cody. Her special guests were boys and girls from St. Stephen's Indian Mission. They were grandchildren of many of the students she had taught in 1890 at the Catholic school located a few miles south of present-day Riverton.

While studying at the university, Milward Simpson was outstanding as an athlete, debater, student and editor. He continued his law studies at Harvard. Simpson financed his education by working as a coal miner, a day laborer, cook on the road construction crew, and a ranch hand. Following World War I, he established a law practice in Cody where he also engaged in the oil business. Alan Simpson, Wyoming's U.S. Senator, is Milward Simpson's son.

WHAT WAS ONE OF THE OFFICIAL WYOMING CENTENNIAL PROJECTS?

The Centennial Messenger, replica of a voyager cruiser used in the early 19th Century, was launched on May 27, 1989 at the historic 1838 Rendezvous site. The event was one of the official projects in celebration of Wyoming's 100th anniversary. Hundreds assembled at the confluence of the Wind and Little Wind Rivers, two miles south of Riverton, to witness the impressive ceremony. The crew consisted of Alan Maybee, Captain; three other men and two women. The Centennial Messenger, loaded with one hundred pounds of beaver pelts, traveled 2,500 miles to St. Louis, following the Wind, Big Horn, Yellowstone, and Missouri Rivers. This was the same route General William H. Ashley, often

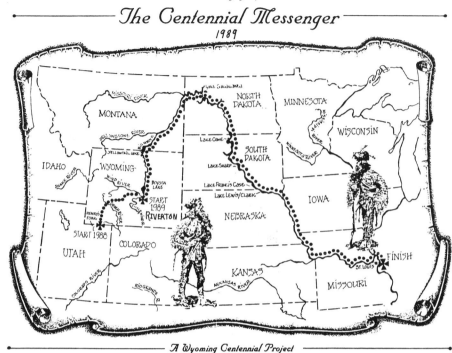

The Voyage of

The Centennial Messenger
1989

A Wyoming Centennial Project

called the "Father of the Rendezvous," used in 1825 when he transported beaver pelts on a voyager cruiser to St. Louis.

IS THE PRESERVATION OF THE 1838 RENDEZVOUS SITE, NEAR RIVERTON, ONE OF THE MANY WYOMING CENTENNIAL LONG-LASTING LEGACIES?

In 1986, the author of this book presented to the Wyoming Centennial Projects director, a plan to preserve the historic 1838 Rendezvous site as Riverton's long-lasting legacy.

50

Four of the nine missionaries, enroute to disputed Oregon country, who attended the 1838 mountain men's summer trade fair, wrote in their diaries about the people and events. Tents, lodges, booths and the area where mules and horses grazed, spread over acres of meadowland on the north side near the confluence of the Wind and Little Wind (Popo Agie) Rivers.

Fred Gowan's classic *The Rocky Mountain Rendezvous: A History of the Fur Trade Rendezvous 1825-1840,* also identifies the historic site where the famous and respected mountain man Jim Bridger and other bearded trappers sold beaver pelts and celebrated with Indian hunters and their squaws.

Riverton businessman John A. Boesch, Jr., chairman, who organized the 1838 Rendezvous Association, and the members, have made long-range plans for the annual four-day celebration in July at the 1838 Rendezvous by the two rivers. The historic site is two miles south of Riverton. In 1989, over 1,000 Wyoming residents and out-of-state tourists stood near the council fire to hear grizzled mountain men in deerskin jackets and trousers tell "tall" tales. They also walked among the tents where Hawken guns, bows and arrows, beaver traps and other 19th century articles were on display.

After soldiers had drunk contraband liquor, Major O'Farrell in 1862 gave orders to condemn and destroy all wagons containing whiskey. The pass is now known as Whiskey Gap.

WHISKEY GAP & OTHER HISTORIC NAMES

HOW DID WHISKEY GAP GET ITS NAME?

The northwest pass in the Green Mountains in present-day Carbon County made history in 1862 when Major Jack O'Farrell, commander of "A" Company, Eleventh Ohio Cavalry, gave the following orders to his officer of the day:

> All wagon trains containing whiskey
> are to be condemned and destroyed!

His order may have been the first official prohibition enforcement action on record in the United States.

Drivers and passengers traveling on the Overland Route from Fort Laramie to South Pass had been attacked and harassed many times by hostile Indians. So as to avoid further trouble, a new route was developed south of the original one that went through the northern part of what is now Colorado. The trail continued over the Laramie Plains, and westward to Green River. At that point the rough road joined the old route near present-day Granger.

Moving equipment, animals and the crew to the stage stations was a long, slow journey, and vulnerable to Indian attacks. The caravan desperately needed protection from hostile Indians, so a detachment of U.S. Army troops from the Eleventh Ohio Calvary accompanied the caravan from Devils Gate Station to the West.

Emigrants also needed Army protection from hostile Indians. One group joined the caravan along with a wagon train that was transporting whiskey, bound for illegal trade with the Indians.

At the end of the first day's journey, the troops camped some ten miles from Devils Gate. Later in the evening, Major O'Farrell noticed that many of the soldiers appeared to be drunk. O'Farrell immediately ordered a search of all the wagons, and the last one contained contraband whiskey. It was then that the commanding officer gave orders to destroy the fire water.

The wagon train was fortunate Indians did not attack that night, with so many inebriated soldiers.

A full account of the event is in Phil Roberts' article, "The 'Good Water' at Whiskey Gap," in the 64-page booklet *More Buffalo Bones*, (Wyoming State Archives, Museums and Historical Department in Cheyenne).

WHAT DOES THE NAME WYOMING MEAN?

Two words from the language of Delaware Indians combine to make "Wyoming." Mary Lou Pence and Laura Homsher in their book, *Ghost Towns of Wyoming*, stated that the name is derived from a combination of two words: *mecheweami-ing*, which means "a land of mountains and valleys alternating."

Another source claims that the name was taken from Wyoming Valley in Pennsylvania, the site of an Indian massacre that became widely known by Campbell's poem, "Gertrude of Wyoming." In the Algonquin language Wyoming means "large prairie place."

WHAT DOES POPO AGIE MEAN?

The name is of Crow origin. *Popo Agie*, (pronounced puh-POH-zuh) means "beginning of waters." At the Sinks, in the Sinks Canyon State Park, several miles south of Lander, in the middle fork of the Popo Agie, the white-capped river whose headwaters are in the Wind River Mountains, gurgles as it flows over boulders. Then it suddenly disappears, or "sinks" into a huge cave as it meanders through an unexplored underground channel. The Popo Agie rises again at a small lake about a mile north of the Sinks.

Large rainbow trout jump for bread people toss into the blue-green water. Tourists are fascinated by the gyrations the trout make as they compete with the other fish for tidbits.

DOES WYOMING HAVE A
TOWN CALLED CENTENNIAL?

There is a town in Wyoming named Centennial. In fact, it's the only village in the U.S. which claims that name. Centennial, located twenty-eight miles west of Laramie in Albany County, sits at the base of the Snowy Range in the Medicine Bow National Forest. In honor of the nation's centennial in 1876, the gold mine, discovered the previous year, was named the Centennial. Later, the community that grew up nearby was also named Centennial.

FOR WHOM WERE JENNY
AND LEIGH LAKES NAMED?

Two glacier-fed lakes in the Teton National Park were named to honor Richard "Beaver Dick" Leigh and his Shoshone wife Jenny. Considered by many to be the last of the mountain men, Beaver Dick lived out his life in the Teton Valley of Jackson Hole in northwestern Wyoming, as well as in the southeastern part of Idaho.

The Englishman became a friend to many famous men, serving as a guide in the 1870s for Dr. F. V. Hayden, head of the United States Geological Survey Expedition which explored the Yellowstone region.

Leigh also guided W. H. Jackson, the first man to photograph the Grand Tetons and the area that would become Yellowstone Park, as well as Nathaniel Lanford, the first superintendent of the national park.

WHY IS THE RIVER AT THE BASE OF THE TETONS CALLED THE SNAKE?

Shoshone Indians called the winding river in the northwestern part of Wyoming, *Yam-pah-pa*, after a plant they found growing along its banks. The Indian women dried and then cooked the yam-pah-pa roots that formed a part of the Shoshone diet.

French trappers, who struggled with the rapids, called the river *La Maudite Riviere Enragee*. Translated into English it means "the accursed mad river."

No one seems to know whether the Snake River was renamed for its twisting, winding course, or for the Shoshone Indians who were called Snake People by neighboring tribes.

HOW DID BADWATER CREEK GET ITS NAME?

For many years the Shoshone people considered the cottonwood-lined banks along the winding stream one of their favorite camping sites. But that changed one spring after a cloudburst caused floodwaters to roar down the valley near the foothills of the Owl Creek Mountains, washing away the tepees of the Shoshone families camped by the creek. Many were drowned before they could escape to higher ground. From that time on, the stream has been known as the Badwater Creek.

Today, some of the largest flocks of sheep in Fremont County graze in the Badwater Creek area.

WHAT'S THE STORY BEHIND
THE NAME RAWHIDE BUTTES?

The most graphic explanation for the name, Rawhide Buttes, located ten miles south of Lusk in Niobrara County, concerns a boastful young Missourian.

In 1849 while on his way with other goldseekers to California, he told the other members of the wagon train that he intended to kill the first Indian he saw.

Soon afterwards the wagon train camped in the east-central section of present Wyoming, where he saw his first native American. The Indian was a woman, but the boastful young man aimed his rifle and shot her.

It was not long before warriors of the woman's tribe surrounded the wagon train. To escape from being killed, the emigrants surrendered the young man to the Indians. Legend says that the Indians skinned the white man alive and then stretched his skin on the blue-black buttes. Hence the name Rawhide Buttes.

HOW DID THE TOWN OF
TEN SLEEP GET ITS NAME?

"Ten Sleep" is from an expression used by Indian people years ago. They measured time and distance in "sleeps" or overnight camps, while traveling from one point to another. The site of Ten Sleep was ten day's travel from the Yellowstone area and the same distance from Fort Laramie; thus the name.

Ten Sleep is near No Wood Creek, named by settlers who were unable to find firewood along its banks.

HOW DID SIGNAL
MOUNTAIN GET ITS NAME?

Signal Mountain, which looks out over the Teton Range, is a memorial for Robert H. Hamilton, who lost his way while hunting in that forested area. The searchers agreed that if Hamilton were found, a signal fire would be lighted on the summit.

Hamilton's body was later found in the Snake River, and the signal fire on the mountain let people know that the hunter had been found.

WHAT WAS THE ORIGINAL NAME
OF THE SHOSHONE RIVER?

Stinking River is the name John Colter gave the odorous stream after he left the Lewis and Clark Expedition in 1806. He traveled alone during the winter months through present-day northwestern Wyoming.

The resourceful adventurer was the first white man to explore the river. Colter called it the Stinking River because of the sulfur which permeated the area. The name was not changed to Shoshone River until the early part of the Twentieth Century.

WHAT WAS FORT WASHAKIE'S
ORIGINAL NAME?

When Washakie, chief of the Shoshone tribe, asked for protection from hostile Indians, Gen. Christopher C. Augur in 1868 built Camp Augur on the present site of Lander. Later the name was changed to Camp Brown for Capt. Frederick Brown, who in 1866 was killed in the Fetterman Massacre. In 1871, the fort was relocated on the Indian reservation and named for Chief Washakie, a friend of the white man.

When Washakie received the silver-trimmed saddle, a gift from President U. S. Grant, he acknowledged the present with the famous words: "Do a kindness to a white man; he feels it in his head, and his tongue speaks. Do a kindness to an Indian, he feels it in his heart; the heart has no tongue."

Fort Washakie was a military post until 1909. It is now the headquarters for the U.S. Indian Service on the Wind River Reservation.

WHY THE NAME FREMONT CANYON?

Captain John C. Fremont in 1842 was unable to float the canyon's rapids in the North Platte river. At another rapids site in the canyon, the boat capsized, losing all records of his journey.

The high-cliffed canyon of many colors is now a part of the Alcova Recreation area, and is supervised by the city of Casper in Natrona County. The Pathfinder Reservoir, named for Fremont who is often called "The Pathfinder," is a few miles to the west of Alcova.

WHAT'S THE ORIGIN OF THE NAME MEDICINE BOW?

The name originates from an expression used by the Indian people who often camped and hunted in the southeastern part of wilderness Wyoming. They found ash along the banks of the rapidly-flowing streams which they used to make bows and arrows. Often the Indians held ceremonial dances in the mountains to cure diseases. The religious dances, the ash and the river were "good medicine." So the river was called Medicine Bow, as well as the mountains. The town of Medicine Bow in Carbon County is famous for the old hotel named for the Virginian, the hero in Owen Wister's famous novel. Published in 1902, the book portrays cowboy life in this western state.

FOR WHOM WAS THE
LARAMIE RIVER NAMED?

The Laramie River was named for Jacques La Ramie, the French-Canadian fur trapper who was killed by Indians about 1820.

Fort Laramie lies within a wide bend of the Laramie River, which flows by on the east and south, thus forming Laramie Plains, then heads toward the Colorado Rockies.

Once a tempestuous waterway, it is almost dry in the late summer months, since much of the water is used to irrigate the productive Wheatland flats, once regarded as desert.

WHICH TOWN WAS MOVED
ACROSS THE BIG HORN RIVER?

Log and clapboard buildings in the town of Worland were hauled across the snow-covered, frozen Big Horn River during the early part of the twentieth century.

Settlers had anticipated that their town on the west side of the river would grow into a prosperous farming community. But in 1906 the Burlington Railroad started laying steel tracks on the east side of the Big Horn.

Undaunted, they started moving buildings to the east side along the tracks. Worland was named in honor of a pioneer, W. H. Worland, who homesteaded in the area in the early 1900s.

The center of a farming and winter stock feeding area, Worland is also the seat of Washakie County. The town often celebrates "Washakie Day" to commemorate the building of the railroad.

HOW DID NEWCASTLE GET ITS NAME?

Often called the "Western Gateway to the Black Hills," the town of Newcastle, county seat of Weston, was named for the English coal port, Newcastle-Upon-Tyne. Many houses in the town, located in the northeastern part of the state, were once built on the sides of steep hills, high above the main street.

WHAT DOES MEETEETSE MEAN?

The Indian word means "place of rest or far away." The town of Meeteetse, some thirty miles south of Cody in Park County, is on the Greybull River. Meeteetse was one of the first settlements in the Big Horn area.

WHO CHANGED THE NAME OF THE SPANISH RIVER TO GREEN RIVER?

General William H. Ashley of St. Louis, Missouri, often called the "Father of the Fur Trappers' Rendezvous," changed the name of the river. In 1824 Ashley decided to rename the Spanish River in honor of one of his partners.

WHY WAS THE TOWN IN FREMONT COUNTY NAMED LANDER?

Frederick W. Lander, a young Army officer during the mid 1800s, was in charge of surveying and building a new route for the Oregon-bound emigrants. The route, from Burnt Ranch on the Sweetwater River, some thirty miles south of the present site of Lander, to the Snake River in Idaho, was surveyed and built during the summer of 1852. It was known as the Lander Cut-off of the Oregon Trail.

In 1884 one of Lander's former scouts and guides. B. F. Lowe, established a townsite in Fremont County, along with E. A. Amoretti and P. P. Dickinson. It was located on the banks of the Popo Agie River. All three men had formerly been living in the gold camp at South Pass City.

Lowe proposed that the new town and post office site be named for his former commander in the Civil War. The town of Lander celebrated its 100th anniversary in 1984.

One of the outstanding events was the eighty-ninth annual Pioneer Days "Pageant of the Old West" parade held on July fourth. Ninety-two entries paraded down the main street, with historical and Indian-built floats of the Arapaho and Shoshone tribes as well as many fine horses, antique automobiles and sheep wagons.

WHICH TOWN IS ON THE NATIONAL REGISTER OF HISTORIC PLACES?

The town of Jay Em in Goshen County is listed in the National Register of Historic Places. Located about thirty miles north of Fort Laramie on Rawhide Creek, the entire town consists of nine structures and nineteen residents.

The name "Jay Em" comes from the initials for James Moore, a cowboy who owned land near the present site of the village. Lake Harris, a homesteader, established Jay Em in 1905.

WHY THE NAME BULL LAKE?

During below-zero weather, the wind whips the snow-covered ice on the glacier-fed lake in the Wind River Mountains. The cold wind lifts the frozen masses and drops them with a thud that sounds like the prolonged roar of an enraged buffalo.

One Shoshone Indian explained that the white buffalo's spirit is roaring with anger, and legend says that hunters chased the bull with the white mantle into the lake where it drowned.

Bull Lake, on the Wind River Reservation in Fremont County, is often called "The Lake That Roars."

HOW DID JACKSON HOLE GET ITS NAME?

David E. Jackson, a trapper working with General William Ashley of St. Louis, caught beaver in the rivers and streams in the area now known as Jackson Hole.

In 1826, he worked with William Sublette and Jedediah S. Smith. Jackson bought out Ashley's interest in the fur trade in the Wyoming wilderness. Later, in 1829 the men sold out to the Rocky Mountain Fur Company.

The word, "Hole," refers to the opening in the mountains which leads to the townsite of Jackson.

FOR WHOM WAS TOGWOTEE PASS NAMED?

Togwotee Pass on the Continental Divide in the Wind River Range, was named for one of the last of the Sheep Eaters.

Togwotee (TOH-guh-tee) was not only a strong Indian leader, he was a feared medicine man and a dependable guide in many Indian battles. At one time he served as a sub-chief under the Shoshone leader, Chief Washakie.

The well known pass, with an elevation of 9,658 feet, is within the Shoshone National Forest. Covered with lodgepole pines, the mountain pass is north of Dubois in Fremont County, and south of Moran Junction. Not far from Togwotee is an off-road lookout where tourists have a breathtaking view of the Grand Tetons.

FOR WHOM WAS LAKE DE SMET NAMED?

For the Belgian-born Jesuit priest who was ordained in the United States in 1827. Father De Smet traveled extensively in the western wilderness during the middle decades of the Nineteenth Century.

The Indians called Father Pierre De Smet "Black Robe," after he had made a strenuous journey with his party over the mountainous country in present-day northern Wyoming. The priest and his followers arrived at the small lake, about six miles long, on Sunday, August 24, 1851.

His companions suggested that the body of water in the Big Horn Mountains be named in his honor. Lake De Smet has since been found to be one of the deepest, natural lakes in the Rocky Mountains.

WHY THE NAME WIND RIVER CANYON?

The scenic high-walled gorge, known as the Wind River Canyon, has been appropriately named. The wind usually blows through the rather narrow chasm, helping to make more ripples in the fast flowing stream.

The river has two names: the Big Wind and the Big Horn. Countless years ago, it cut through the Owl Creek Range and carved the deep canyon that is almost as varied in color as the coat belonging to David, the shepherd king of the Old Testament.

Indian people called the glacier-fed stream the Wind River because the wind sometimes whistles and even howls. The headwaters are in the Wind River Range, north of the rustic, western town of Dubois in Fremont County.

Halfway through the Wind River Canyon, the river is known as the Big Horn, for the bighorn sheep, with creamy white rumps and massive coiled horns, which live on mountain slopes with sparse growths of trees.

Fossils, artifacts and rocks are in the magnificent canyon, with cedar trees and wild flowers, including yucca plants. The rock formations range from the Precambrian period, the oldest and longest division of geologic time, to the Mesozoic period, the third era of geologic time.

The sixteen-mile paved road on U.S. Highway 20 has several tunnels. The road follows the river through the Wind River Canyon, south of Thermopolis. The well-known resort town with the world-famous hot springs and large buffalo herd, is located on the west bank of the Big Horn River in Hot Springs County.

"The Wedding of the Waters," one of the most dramatic pageants in Wyoming, tells the reason the Indian people sold the hot springs to the white people. The annual event, held in the Hot Springs State Park in Thermopolis, is observed the first weekend in August.

The Shoshone Indians from the Wind River Reservation set up their white tepees in the park by the mineral springs. They are the main performers in the pageant, and wear their beaded, deerskin costumes, which are often decorated with bright feathers and sequins.

The Big Wind-Big Horn River is one of the important sources of water to irrigate the thousands of acres in the once-dry sagebrush land. The Big Wind-Big Horn eventually joins the Yellowstone River, then the Missouri and finally the Mississippi.

HOW DID SOUTH PASS CITY GET IT'S NAME?

The first gold mining camp in wilderness Wyoming, located in the foothills at the southern end of the Wind River Range, was called South Pass City in the late 1860s. Now known as the South Pass City State Historic Site, it is some fifteen miles from the famous South Pass.

Thousands of men, women and children, in covered wagons, on horseback and even on foot, traveled over the Continental Divide at South Pass.

Probably the most famous resident to live with her family in South Pass City was Esther Hobart Morris, the first woman justice of the peace in the United States. She was commissioned on February 14, 1870. At the far east end of South Pass Avenue is the reconstructed Morris cabin, considered by many as symbolizing the women's suffrage movement, not only in Wyoming, but in the nation. Members of the non-profit Friends of South Pass often serve as guides. They also are in charge of the sales of books, postcards and old-fashion candy at the Smith-Sherlock store. The funds are used to help pay the expenses of interns and researchers.

WHAT ARE THE NAME ORIGINS FOR WYOMING'S TWENTY-THREE COUNTIES?

(Adapted from the *Wyoming Blue Book*, Vol. III, edited by Virginia Cole Trenholm)

Albany:

Charles Bradley, a member of the Dakota legislature, chose the name Albany, capital of New York, where he had formerly lived. The county was organized during January of 1869. Laramie is the county seat.

Big Horn:

Hundreds of brown and grayish-brown big horn sheep, with massive coiled horns, at one time climbed the Big Horn Mountains. The county was organized June 4, 1897, with Basin serving as the county seat.

Campbell:

This county was named for two men with the surname of Campbell. John A. Campbell was Wyoming's first territorial governor, from April 15, 1869 until March 1, 1875, when he resigned. Campbell had served as assistant secretary of war in President Grant's cabinet before becoming the territorial governor. The county was also named for Robert Campbell, a member of the William Ashley expedition which explored wilderness Wyoming during the 1820s. The county of Campbell was organized May 23, 1911. Gillette is the county seat.

Carbon:

There are rich coal deposits in this county. The Union Pacific Railroad once had a mining camp at Carbon. After mine activity proved more prosperous in Hanna, the city of Carbon became a ghost town. The county of Carbon was organized in January 1869, with Rawlins as the county seat.

Converse:

Amasa R. Converse, Cheyenne banker and stockman, was honored when the county was named for him. He served as treasurer for Wyoming Territory from 1877 to 1879, and, at one time, ran cattle under some twenty-eight brands. Douglas is the seat of this county, organized May 21, 1888.

Crook:

The county was named for General George Crook who led the second Powder River expedition against the Indians. Crook County was organized January 2, 1885. Sundance is the county seat.

Fremont:

Capt. John Charles Fremont, often called "The Pathfinder," explored the wilderness during the mid-19th Century. He climbed one of the tallest peaks in the Wind River Range, and unfurled the American flag. He named the snow-covered summit Fremont Peak, but years later it was renamed Woodrow Wilson Peak. Fremont County celebrated its centennial with year-long festivities in 1984. Organized May 6, 1884, Lander is the county seat.

Goshen:

There are two explanations for the name of this county. Goshen was probably derived from Guache's Hole (Goshen Hole). The depression in the plateau in east-central Wyoming was named for the French trapper, Gosche, who set his traps for beaver in the area. The other explanation is that the county was named for the fertile land in Egypt in the biblical "land of Goshen." Goshen was organized January 6, 1913, with Torrington as the county seat.

Hot Springs:

Shoshones and Arapahos sold a few acres of land on their reservation to the government in the now famous mineral hot springs in the city of Thermopolis. Hot Springs County was established January 6, 1913, with Thermopolis as its seat.

Johnson:

Originally called Pease, the county's name was changed to Johnson by the Legislative Assembly in 1879. A Cheyenne attorney, E. P. Johnson served as territorial librarian from 1871 until 1873. Buffalo heads the county that was organized May 10, 1881.

Laramie:

The legendary French-Canadian Jacques La Ramie hunted the tributaries of the North Platte in the southeastern part of present-day Wyoming in about 1820. One early historian, C. G. Coutant, claims La Ramie was killed by Indians along the banks of the river now called the Laramie. His name has also been given to a military post, a river, a peak, a mountain range, a county, a city and a section of the Wyoming Plains. In January 1867 when Laramie county was organized, it was in Dakota Territory. Cheyenne is the county seat.

Lincoln:

Named for Abraham Lincoln, the sixteenth president of the U.S., the county was organized January 6, 1913, with Kemmerer as its seat.

Natrona:

The county was named for the soda deposits (natron) found in that part of Central Wyoming. Casper is the county seat. Natrona County was organized April 12, 1890, by cutting Carbon County in half.

Niobrara:

Named for the Indian tribe that frequented the area, "Niobrara" comes from the Omaha Indian word which means "flat or broad river." Organized January 8, 1913, Lusk is the county seat.

Park:

The county was named for Yellowstone, the first national park in the U.S. Park County was organized January 9, 1911, and is located east of the famous park. Cody is the county seat.

Platte:

The southeastern county is named for the river that winds its way through a number of Wyoming counties. Platte is a French word which means "shallow" or "dull." The county was organized January 6, 1913; Wheatland is the county seat.

Sheridan:

This northern Wyoming county was named in honor of General Philip Sheridan who served during the American Civil War. Organized May 11, 1888, the city of Sheridan is its county seat. In 1903, Sheridan had thirty saloons, six churches and two opera houses.

Sublette:

Fur trader, Capt. William Sublette and a party of men took five head of cattle to the Wind River Rendezvous in 1830. The last of the twenty-three counties to be organized on January 2, 1923, Sublette's county seat is in Pinedale. The elaborate pageant, "The Green River Rendezvous," held in Pinedale, is an annual July event.

Sweetwater:

This county was named for the river whose headwaters are in the Wind River Mountains. Created December 27, 1867 by Dakota laws, the county was called Carter for Judge W. A. Carter, early settler of Fort Bridger. The name was changed to Sweetwater by the Legislative Assembly in 1869.

Teton:

French trappers described the highest peaks of the mountain range as *Trois Tetons*, which means "Three Pinnacles." The Tetons are considered one of the most spectacular ranges in the nation. Organized December 2, 1922, Jackson, the county seat, is south of the Teton National Park.

Uinta:

The county is named for the Uintah Indians. The Uinta (Ute) mountain range is unique in that it runs east and west. The county was organized April 7, 1870, with Evanston as its seat.

Washakie:

Chief Washakie, who died in 1900, was the Shoshone tribal leader for more than fifty years. The county, organized January 6, 1913, was named in his honor. Worland is the county seat.

Weston:

The county was named for Dr. Jefferson B. Weston, the geologist-engineer who was influential in the building of the Chicago, Burlington & Quincy Railroad in Wyoming. Weston was organized May 16, 1890. Newcastle is the county seat.

"WE WON'T COME IN WITHOUT OUR WOMEN"

DID THE HISTORIC TELEGRAM WYOMING LEGISLATORS SENT IN 1890, IMPLY: "WE WON'T COME IN WITHOUT OUR WOMEN?"

The Wyoming Territorial Legislature was in session in Cheyenne in 1890 when members of the 51st Congress in the national capital were arguing for and against statehood for Wyoming. Women suffrage was the controversial issue. The Wyoming Constitution, ratified the previous year, on November 5, 1889, provided for equal rights for both male and female citizens.

The Honorable Joseph M. Carey, Wyoming's delegate in Congress, telegraphed the legislators in Cheyenne, expressing his fears that statehood would be denied unless the suffrage clause in the Constitution was abandoned.

Members of the Wyoming Legislature, all men, "without equivocation or delay," telegraphed in reply:

> We will remain out of the union a
> hundred years rather than go in
> without women suffrage.

In other words:

> We won't come in without our
> women.

This statement expresses the message contained in the historic 1890 telegram.

Without curtailing the rights or privileges of any of its citizens, Wyoming Territory, on July 10, 1890, was admitted as the 44th state in the Union.

Twenty-one years before, in 1869, Wyoming was the first government in the U.S. to grant women the right to vote and hold office.

In January, 1918, President Woodrow Wilson endorsed the proposed 19th Amendment to the Constitution, giving suffrage, nationwide, to women. In September of that same year, Senator John B. Kendrick of Wyoming presented to the Senate arguments in favor of suffrage for all women in the United States. In his speech, printed in the September 30, 1918 edition of the *Congressional Record,* Kendrick quoted the historic statement Wyoming legislators telegraphed to Washington, D.C. in 1890:

> We will remain out of the union a
> hundred years rather than go in
> without women suffrage.

The 19th Amendment, giving nationwide suffrage to women, was proposed by Congress on June 4, 1919. Ratification was certified by the Secretary of State on August 26, 1920.

WHO WERE THE FIRST WHITE WOMEN IN WILDERNESS WYOMING?

In 1836, Narcissa Prentiss Whitman and Eliza Hart Spalding, recent brides of missionaries, not only were the first white women in the wilderness now known as Wyoming, they were the first fair-haired ladies attending the mountain men's summer trade fair, popularly called the rendezvous. They were also the first white American women to cross over the Continental Divide at South Pass in the Rocky Mountains.

These two women from the eastern states have the distinction of being the first white females to travel across the North American continent, having traveled from the Atlantic seaboard to the Pacific Ocean. Enroute to establish a Protestant mission in the Pacific Northwest, Dr. Marcus Whitman and his wife Narcissa, the Reverend Henry H. Spalding and his wife Eliza, and William H. Gray met the supply train on May 24, 1836, at Loup Fork Missouri. The caravan was headed for the central Rockies, guided by the experienced mountain man, Thomas Fitzpatrick. There were the two women, 70 men and some 400 animals, mostly mules in the caravan. The American women rode sidesaddle most of the time on this long journey.

Six weeks later, on Wednesday, July 6, 1836, the caravan arrived at the Green River (Siskeedee-Agie) Rendezvous. The extensive meadowland, where beaver trappers, Indian hunters and tradesmen often assembled for the summer trade fairs, was in the vicinity of Fort Bonneville, near the present site of Daniel in Sublette County on the west side of the Wind River Range.

Mountain men, who trapped beavers in the rivers and streams were overjoyed to see the two gentlewomen. The Indian braves, their squaws and children were even more fascinated, since this was the first time they had ever seen ladies with white skin.

The missionaries conducted Sunday services at the trade fair. Then on July 18, 1836, they traveled with the Hudson's Bay Company on the last lap of their journey.

That fall the missionaries arrived in wilderness Washington where they founded a mission at Waiilatpu, now in the Whitman National Monument, near present-day Walla Walla. Shortly after they arrived at their destination, Narcissa Whitman wrote:

This was an unheard of journey for females!

75

A monument, erected in Wyoming to honor the Whitmans and Spaldings, is about fifteen miles from the South Pass City State Historic Site, at the southern pass, later known as the "Gateway to the West."

HOW MANY WHITE WOMEN ATTENDED THE 1838 WIND RIVER RENDEZVOUS?

Four American women, wives of Protestant missionaries, arrived in time for the mountain men's trade fair in the Wind River Basin near the present town of Riverton.

A notice, written in charcoal and tacked on a storehouse door near Fort Bonneville on the Green River, told the following:

> Come to Poposua on Wind River and
> you will find plenty trade, whiskey
> and white women.

After reading the notice, beaver trappers, who had been uncertain where the 1838 rendezvous would be held, then headed their horses, mules and pack trains for the summer trade fair on the other side of the Wind River Range.

The four white women, who attended the rendezvous at the confluence of the Wind and Little Wind (Popo Agie) Rivers, were:

> Myra Fairbanks Eells
> Mary Richardson Walker
> Sarah Gilbert White Smith and
> Mary Augusta Dix Gray.

The missionaries arrived on Saturday, June 23, 1838, with the supply train from Westport, Missouri. There were 75 people and 150 horses and mules in the caravan. Also at the rendezvous were August Johann Sutter, who later built Fort Sutter in California where gold was discovered in 1849; and

Sir William Drummond Stewart on his last visit to the Wind River Mountains before returning to his home in Scotland.

Journals written by the missionaries give valuable details about the rendezvous, one of the last ever held in the Rockies. Those who kept diaries were Mary Walker, Cushing Eells and his wife Myra; Asa B. Smith and his wife Sarah. They also wrote long letters while traveling to the Oregon country to Christianize the Indians.

Like Narcissa Whitman and Eliza Spalding, who were greeted with a noisy reception by the mountain men and Indian trappers at the 1836 rendezvous on the Green River, so were these women honored in a similar, somewhat crude manner.

At the 1838 Wind River Rendezvous, one of the mountain men displayed the scalp of a Blackfoot Indian in an attempt to impress the wives of four American missionaries. The women were shocked.

Myra Eells wrote the following, Thursday, July 5, 1838:

> ...Capt. Bridger's company comes in about 10 o'clock with drums and firing – an apology for a scalp dance. After they had given Capt. Drip's company a shout, 15 or 20 mountain men and Indians came to our tent with drumming, firing and dancing. If I might make a comparison, I should say that they looked like emissaries of the Devil worshipping their own master. They had the scalp of a Blackfoot Indian, which they carried for color, all rejoicing in the fate of the Blackfoot Indian, in consequence of the smallpox...

WHERE WAS SACAJAWEA BURIED?

Historians have never settled the question of Sacajawea's final resting place, or when she died. The young Shoshone woman has been called the "Bird Woman" by English speaking people. However, that translation has been challenged. There are also various spellings of her name.

As a young girl, Sacajawea was captured and sold to a Mandan Indian and eventually traded to Toussaint Charbonneau. As one of his wives and the only woman on the Lewis and Clark Expedition (1804-1806), she proved an invaluable guide and interpreter when the explorers and their party reached the upper Missouri River and the mountains where she found her brother. Carrying her baby son in a cradleboard on her back she endured the long rugged, journey over the Rockies and west to the Pacific Ocean. The party then made its way back to a Mandan village in the Dakotas.

Some historians claim Sacajawea was born in 1812, and died at the age of twenty-five of "putrid fever" at Fort Manuel Lisa in North Dakota. Others, including Shoshone people, claim that Sacajawea died in 1884 on their reservation in Wyoming and was buried in an Indian mound near the Wind River Mountains.

In 1943, the Wyoming Society of the Daughters of the American Revolution placed a granite monument at the Sacajawea Cemetery, south of Fort Washakie, on the Wind River Reservation.

Sacajawea is one of the best-known women in American history. Poets and writers have told her story and painters and sculptors have immortalized her on stone and canvas.

WHAT GOVERNMENT WAS THE FIRST TO GIVE WOMEN THE RIGHT TO VOTE?

When Wyoming was still a territory, male representatives, elected to the First Territorial Legislature in 1869 at Cheyenne, voted on a bill of worldwide importance.

The politicians adopted "An Act to Grant Women of Wyoming Territory the Right of Suffrage and to Hold Office," and Territorial Governor John A. Campbell signed the bill on December 10, 1869.

WHO IS THE "FATHER" OF WOMEN'S SUFFRAGE?

William H. Bright, the Democrat from South Pass City, introduced the women's suffrage bill in the Council, later called the Senate, at the First Territorial Legislature held in Cheyenne during the fall of 1869. Bright, a miner and saloon owner in the gold mining camp, was also the first president of the Council.

When asked the reasons he introduced the womens' suffrage bill, Bright explained that he knew it was a new and live issue, but he felt that it was just. He also said that he was determined to use all the influence he had to see that the bill was passed. His wife Julia Bright believed women should have equal rights with men.

WHO GRUDGINGLY DRANK A TOAST TO WOMEN'S SUFFRAGE?

At Wyoming's first territorial legislative session, members of the Council and House of Representatives voted on the women's suffrage act, and Governor John A. Campbell signed the bill into law on December 10, 1869.

Many of the legislators did not take too kindly to the law, but they raised their glasses and drank to the toast:

> To the lovely ladies, once our superiors, now our equals.

WHO WAS THE FIRST WOMAN JUSTICE OF THE PEACE IN THE WORLD?

In 1870 Esther Morris of South Pass City was commissioned Justice of the Peace in the gold mining camp where she lived. She held office eight and one-half months, and handled twenty-six cases.

Dr. T. A. Larson, author of *History of Wyoming* wrote "...the consensus at the time and in later years was that a Wyoming woman met the test of public office." Mrs. Morris had been commissioned by Edward M. Lee, secretary of the Territory of Wyoming.

Among the interesting buildings in South Pass City is Esther Morris' home. She was chosen as Wyoming's outstanding deceased citizen, and her image is in the Statutory Hall at the U.S. Capital in Washington, D.C., and also at Wyoming's capitol entrance in Cheyenne.

WHO WAS ONE OF THE FIRST WOMEN TO VOTE IN A GENERAL ELECTION?

One of the first women to cast her ballot in the Territory of Wyoming; in fact, in the entire world, during a general election was Eliza A. Swain of Laramie. She was a gentle, 70-year-old, white-haired homemaker, who was Quakerish in appearance.

The book, *Women of Wyoming*, (Cora M. Beach, editor), contains the following information about the historic event:

> On the eve of the election, Tuesday, September 6, 1870, she (Eliza Swain) put on a clean white apron, one of the belted kind tied in the back, with a shawl on her shoulders, a hat and with a little tin pail, went to the polls. She carried the pail for the purpose of getting yeast, possibly for what was called a "starter" in the early days.
>
> Judge M. C. Brown of Laramie, a resident of that town and a practicing attorney, in those days before the famous "first jury" and who has first-hand information of the events of that early day, is authority for the statement that she arrived at the polls early and because she was elderly and so well and favorably known, they thought it would be a great honor to bestow on her, to allow her to be the first voter, and hence they opened the polls a little earlier than the hour set, and allowed her to vote first...

WHAT TERRITORY OR STATE
HAD THE FIRST WOMEN JURORS?

The territory of Wyoming had the first women jurors. A few months after passage of the suffrage act in Wyoming, women served on grand and petit juries in Laramie, starting in the months of March and April, 1870.

Before women served on juries, the male jurors often interrupted their discussions of the court trial with drinking and gambling. But when women began serving on juries, those practices ended. In fact, smoking and chewing tobacco were also not allowed while men and women jurors were on duty.

It's interesting to note that female jurors had a tendency to convict defendants and to recommend heavy sentences more often than their male counterparts.

However, in 1871, new judges on the bench stopped using women on juries. What reason did they use? They claimed that jury service for females was not an "adjunct of suffrage."

Seventy-eight years later, on February 19, 1949, the "Women Jury Law," (original House Bill No. 40), granted women the right to serve on a jury.

WHO WAS THE FIRST WYOMING WOMAN
TO GO INTO THE CATTLE BUSINESS?

She was Margaret Burke Heenan of Miner's Delight, a resident of the gold mining camp in the 1870s. Long abandoned, Miner's Delight is located near Atlantic City in Fremont County.

Margaret Burke was three months old when her parents brought her from Dublin, Ireland to the United States. Years later she worked as a seamstress in Cheyenne, where in 1867, she married Michael Heenan, a construction contractor for the Union Pacific Railroad. Excited by the gold rush in the South Pass City-Atlantic City region, they moved to Miner's Delight near the Wind River Mountains.

Then tragedy struck, leaving Margaret a widow when her husband, while working as a teamster, was ambushed and brutally scalped by Indians at Twin Creek Hill on September 17, 1872. He was bringing a wagonload of hay from the Lander Valley.

Not long after their daughter was born prematurely, the widowed mother of three opened up a boarding house in her cabin near Spring Gulch. Her boarders were prospectors, freighters and transient travelers. The miners paid Mrs. Heenan for their meals with gold nuggets that she placed in a large pickle jar. When the jar in her kitchen was full, she traded the nuggets for some cattle.

It wasn't long before she had a fair-sized herd grazing in the meadowland along Spring Gulch, near the mining camp, and her cattle were branded with a "Circle H" in memory of her late husband.

On August 16, 1875 she married Peter P. Dickinson, who was later one of the founding fathers of the town of Lander, established in 1884. The Dickinsons lived on Main Street where they managed the Cottage Hotel. The couple also ran cattle in the Wind River Mountains, in an area now called Dickinson Park.

Margaret Dickinson organized the first public school in Lander. She secured a land grant for both the Episcopal and Catholic churches in Lander, as well as getting land for the Episcopal Church in Shoshoni. She also organized the first Sunday School in Lander.

Mrs. Dickinson was the first woman to serve on the Lander School Board, and was often a delegate to the Wyoming State Democratic conventions. On two occasions she was the alternate to the national Democratic conventions.

She gave the three Dobler girls, Virginia, Lavinia and Frances, a heifer to raise. Dolly lived in the barn in back of the Dobler home in Riverton, at Monroe Avenue and Third Street. Shortly after the girls' aunt Gertrude Lavinia Dobler, arrived in Lander to teach in the high school, she married William, Peter and Margaret Dickinson's only son.

WHO WAS THE FIRST WOMAN ELECTED TO A STATE OFFICE?

Estelle Reel, born in Pittsfield, Illinois, was thirty-six years old in 1894, when she was elected to the post of superintendent of public instruction in Wyoming. A Republican, she had the honor of being the first woman in the country elected to a state office. Another interesting fact is that Estelle Reel received, in 1894, the largest number of votes ever given a candidate in the state of Wyoming.

She took over the duties as head of the state education office on January 7, 1895, serving until January 27, 1898. She resigned to accept another responsible position when President William McKinley appointed her National Superintendent of Indian Schools. She was unanimously confirmed in 1898 by the United States Senate.

WHO WAS THE FIRST WOMAN ELECTED TO A STATE LEGISLATURE IN THE U.S.?

Mary G. Bellamy a Democrat from Laramie represented Albany County in the House of Representative in 1911. She was the first woman elected to a state legislature in this country. Two years later Anna B. Miller of Albany County and Nettie Truax of Crook and Campbell counties, both Democrats, served in the 1913 House of Representatives.

Mary Bellamy went to Washington to represent Wyoming women during the national campaign for the Nineteenth Amendment, the national suffrage bill.

WHO MAY HAVE BEEN THE FIRST WOMAN MAYOR IN THE UNITED STATES?

In 1911 the small Western town of Dayton, located northwest of Sheridan, attracted considerable attention by electing Susan Wissler its mayor. Dayton residents, at that time, claimed that Mrs. Wissler was the first woman mayor in this country, but the honor has since been disputed.

WHO DRAFTED THE BILL FOR THE STATE FLOWER?

Dr. Grace Raymond Hebard of the University of Wyoming drafted the bill. She also personally employed the New York artist, Margaret Armstrong, to paint a picture of the Indian paintbrush. The bill had been recommended for passage by the Laramie Chapter of the Daughters of the American Revolution. (*Wyoming Blue Book*, Vol. II).

The Indian paintbrush became the state flower on Tuesday, January 31, 1917, the same day the Fourteenth Legislature adopted the Wyoming state flag, designed by Vera Keays of Buffalo.

George F. Dobler, lawyer from Riverton and the father of the author of this book, at that session was serving as chairman of the Judiciary Committee in the House of Representatives. He voted for the state flower, the Wyoming paintbrush.

In the reference book, *A Field Guide to Rocky Mountain Wildflowers*, written by John J. Craighead, Frank C. Craighead, Jr., and Ray J. Davis, the scientists list the flower's botanical name, *Castilleja linariaefolia*, as the Wyoming paintbrush. Other names for the flower are painted-cup and Wyoming painted cup.

When in bloom in June, July and the first part of August, the highly colored bracts and upper leaves as well as the red or scarlet leaf-like bracts below each tiny yellowish green flower make a brilliant impression on the landscape.

WHO WAS THE FIRST WOMAN FOUND GUILTY IN COURT OF RUSTLING?

In November, 1919, Anna Richey was found guilty of rustling in the area near Kemmerer. Although some of the ranchers described her as "thirty, purty, and full of life," a Lincoln County judge sentenced her to prison.

She was known in Southwestern Wyoming as "Queen Anna" because she sat well in the saddle, handling her horse with dignity and grace. A woman of culture, Anna Richey was the daughter of a wealthy rancher. She'd had many suitors before she married a teacher. She was later divorced.

Some of the ranchers considered Anna too ambitious for a woman, and some were aware that she was impatient to enlarge her herd of cattle. In July, 1919, Anna Richey rounded up thirty-two head of cattle that did not belong to her. At Fossil, not far from the now famous Fossil Butte, she loaded them onto railroad cars and shipped them to Omaha, Nebraska.

So Anna was accused of rustling. On the way to the trial, she was shot by a masked rider. She was hospitalized and recovered in time to be found guilty of rustling and altering eight brands. Sentenced to six years in the state penitentiary, she was free on bond to wind up her ranch business, but died suddenly while working with her hired man.

Rumors said she had been poisoned, and ranchers in the Ham's Fork area claimed that she had been talking to a stranger the day before she died. But the reason for her death still remains a mystery.

WHO DESIGNED THE STATE FLAG?

Verna Keays of Buffalo designed the state flag. Thirty-seven designs were submitted in the contest conducted by the Daughters of the American Revolution. In March 1, 1919 the flag's designer donated the original sketch of the state flag to the Wyoming Historical Department.

The artist wrote the following legend about the Wyoming state flag:

> The Great Seal of the State of
> Wyoming is the heart of the flag.
>
> The seal of the bison represents the
> truly western custom of branding.
> The bison was once 'monarch of the
> plains.'
>
> The red border represents the red
> man, who knew and loved our coun-
> try long before any of us were here;
> also, the blood of the pioneers who
> gave their lives reclaiming the soil.
>
> White is an emblem of purity and
> uprightness over Wyoming.
>
> Blue, which is found in the bluest of
> blue Wyoming skies and the distant
> mountains, has through the ages
> been significant of fidelity, justice
> and virility.
>
> And finally, the red, the white and
> the blue of the flag of the state of
> Wyoming are the colors of the great-
> est flag in all the world, the stars and
> stripes of the United States of
> America.

The Wyoming state flag was adopted by the legis-lature, January 31, 1917. The Indian paintbrush became the state flower at the same time.

WHO WAS THE FIRST WOMAN
GOVERNOR IN THE UNITED STATES?

Nellie Tayloe Ross of Wyoming was elected to fill
the last two years of her husband's unexpired term.
Governor William B. Ross died a month before the
general election of 1924. Mrs. Ross took the oath of
office as governor of Wyoming on Monday, January
5, 1925. A few days later, Miriam Wallace Ferguson,
also elected in 1924, became the first woman governor of Texas, and like Mrs. Ross, was a Democrat
who served from 1925-1927.

Mrs. Ross also has the distinction of being the first
woman director of the U.S. Mint in Washington,
D.C. The appointment was made in April, 1933.

Two of Wyoming's "first ladies," Thyra Thomson,
first woman secretary of state, and Nellie Tayloe
Ross, then 92 years old, attended the Yellowstone
Park Centennial in 1972.

DO WOMEN SERVE ON TRIBAL COUNCILS
ON THE WIND RIVER RESERVATION?

The Arapaho and Shoshone tribes permitted
women to serve on the two tribal councils before the
Wyoming Supreme Court unanimously upheld the
constitutionality of the "Women on Jury Act" passed
by the state legislature in 1949.

WHO WAS THE FIRST WOMAN ELECTED
TO THE SHOSHONE TRIBAL COUNCIL?

In 1930 Irene Kinnear Mead, granddaughter of
Jim Baker, famous American trapper and mountain
man originally from Illinois, was the first Shoshone
woman elected to the Tribal Council. At the meet-
ings held on the Wind River Reservation, Council
members decide on matters pertaining to the several
thousand Shoshone men, women and children, most

of whom live in comfortable wooden homes, not tepees, in sight of the Wind River Mountains.

The Shoshones and Arapahoes receive annual royalty payments for oil produced on their reservation. Most Indian families drive pickup trucks, vans and passenger cars to get supplies in the neighboring towns, Riverton and Lander in Fremont County. This is in sharp contrast to the wagons drawn by horses the Indian people used for transportation not too many decades ago.

The Wyoming town of Kinnear was named for Irene Kinnear Meads's father, Napaleon Bonaparte Kinnear, who owned a ranch in Fremont County.

WHEN DID NELL SCOTT BEGIN HER TERM ON THE ARAPAHO TRIBAL COUNCIL?

In 1937 Nell Scott began her first term on the Arapaho Tribal Council. She was the second woman on the Wind River Indian Reservation in Fremont County to be elected to one of the two tribal councils. Irene Kinnear Mead, a member of the Shoshone Tribe, was the first.

Nell Scott has the distinction of having been listed on both tribal rolls. Because of a technicality she was dropped by the Shoshones. Later she was placed on the Arapaho tribal roll by Chief Yellow Calf. Mrs. Scott was 83 years old in 1974. At that time she had served for three decades on the Arapaho Tribal Council. Her white bungalow home at Fort Washakie had a large well-cared-for lawn and a rose garden. East of where Nell Scott lived, is the old military cemetery by the Little Wind River where Chief Washakie, leader of the Shoshone Tribe for fifty years, is buried. When Nell Scott's mother was a small child, she was found on a battlefield, having been abandoned by Indian warriors.

WHO WAS WYOMING'S
FIRST POET LAUREATE?

Peggy Simson Curry of Casper was honored as Wyoming's first poet laureate in January, 1981 by Ed Herschler, governor of Wyoming. Her book length narrative poem, *Red Wind of Wyoming*, about the Johnson County War in 1892 near Buffalo, was adapted as a radio drama in 1969 by Frank Parman. The author, who had been reading Asa Mercer's *Banditti of the Plains*, conceived the idea for her poem while sitting in Casper's Elbow Room in the Henning Hotel.

Johnson County was invaded by "regulators," stockmen and Texas gunmen who tried to put a stop to rustling with armed force. The Johnson County War continues to be one of the most controversial and publicized events in the state's history.

Wyoming Writers honored Peggy Simson Curry with two "Emmie Mygatt" awards for outstanding service to writers within the state. Western Writers of America presented her with two "Spur Awards" in the fields of juvenile and adult fiction.

She considered *So Far From Spring* her best novel. This Western novel as well as *The Oil Patch* and *Fire in the Water* have been translated into many languages.

The Casper resident served as chairman of the Wyoming Bicentennial Commission in 1976. Her life has been described in Jean Mead's book, *Wyoming in Profile*.

WHO WAS GIVEN THE TITLE "GRAND
LADY OF THE BOZEMAN TRAIL?"

Elsa Spear Byron, born near Big Horn, and the descendant of one of Wyoming's first families, was given the title, "Grand Lady of the Bozeman Trail" by National Geographic in its 1979 edition of the book, *Trails West*. She was named in 1976 as one of three outstanding artist-photographers by the University of Wyoming. Elsa Spear Byron was also the recipient of the Trustees Award in 1982 from the National Cowboy Hall of Fame in Oklahoma City.

Author of three books on Wyoming history, she is the Big Horn area's authority on the Bozeman Trail, Fort Phil Kearney and other regional history. She was honored by Governor Ed Herschler on June 2, 1984, when he proclaimed "Elsa Spear Byron Day," and by Wyoming Writers at their workshop in Sheridan on the same day. Dr. Gene M. Gressley, then archivist and head of the Western History Research Center of the University of Wyoming, also spoke of her contributions to the state.

Her father, Willis M. Spear and three other family members moved to the Big Horn area from Montana in 1883, bringing along 100 head of cattle and 175 horses. In 1923, the Spear family opened Spear-O-Wigwam in the Big Horn Mountains to cater to the dude trade.

Interest in Elsa's photography soared that year when she led a group of women from a September mountain blizzard, blacking their faces with charcoal, tearing up gunny sacks for their feet, while snapping photographs along the way. By Christmas, seventy of the pictures had been sold, and Elsa was on her way to a career in photography.

WHICH WOMAN IN 1984 HELD THE SECOND HIGHEST STATE OFFICE IN WYOMING?

Thyra Thomson, elected Wyoming's first woman secretary of state in 1962, consecutively held the second highest office in Wyoming for more than twenty years, as of November 1984.

Mrs. Thomson, whose husband was a U.S. senator-elect at the time of his death in 1960, was reelected secretary of state in 1966. She received the "biggest majority ever received in Wyoming by a candidate for a partisan office," according to the *Wyoming Blue Book,* Volume III (1974).

HAS THE WIND RIVER RESERVATION
EVER HAD WOMEN FIRE FIGHTERS?

The 1974 Sho-Arap Fire Fighters School at Fort
Washakie trained its first women fire fighters. Of
the 233 trainees, forty-two were women. Forty
were Arapahoes and two were Shoshones.

WHAT'S A JACKALOPE?
&
OTHER WESTERN WORDS

WHAT'S A JACKALOPE?

It's a furry animal that is shaped like a large jack rabbit with curved horns of a buck antelope. The trapper Ron Black was the first man to "see" a jackalope in Wyoming in 1851, so people say. When Black told his drinking cronies about the unusual creature, they shouted "LIAR!"

There are jackalopes in this Western state, but they don't hop like a jack rabbit or run like an antelope. They are statues, including one in the town of Douglas, where residents celebrate "Jackalope Day."

The jackalope has the long ears of a jack rabbit and the horns of a buck antelope. This unusual animal is found in statue-form in a number of Wyoming towns, but not on the prairie.

93

WHAT NAME IN THE WEST WAS ONCE SYNONYMOUS WITH COFFEE?

Arbuckles. Years ago many Westerners considered it redundant to use the words Arbuckles and coffee together. When describing the "ariosa" coffee, the owners of Arbuckle Bros. Coffee Company of New York City stated:

> The glazing, composed of eggs and sugar, not only retains the full strength and aroma of our coffee, but gives to it a richness of flavor unknown to other coffees; besides it saves the expense of eggs used in settling unglazed coffee.

WHAT'S A NESTER?

In the Western part of the United States, a nester was a squatter, farmer or homesteader who settled in cattle-grazing country. During the late Nineteenth Century, cattlemen and nesters were in conflict. One of the most historic events in Wyoming's history pertains to the Johnson County War in 1892.

WHAT'S SISKEEDEE-AGIE?

The Crow Indian word for the glacier-fed Green River, in the southwestern section of Wyoming, means Prairie Hen River. There are at least four variations in the spelling of Siskeedee-Agie, including *Siskadee, Sheetska dee, Siskedo-azzeah* and *Seedskedee-agie*.

WHAT'S A CHINOOK?

A chinook is a warm, moist southwest wind which descends from the eastern slopes of the Rocky Mountains. Chinook is also the name of a North

American Indian tribe living along the Columbia River.

Wyoming cattlemen, as well as other stockmen in the West, welcome a good chinook, especially if it comes from the north, melting the snow, thus allowing the cattle and sheep to reach grass.

WHAT'S A BOOTHILL?

Also known as a boot graveyard, boothill is a cemetery on the top of a hill near a frontier town in Wyoming, as well as in other camps and towns in the West. No doubt the word is associated with the man's wish to die with his boots on. Stephen Vincent Benet in "The Ballad of William Sycamore" wrote:

> I died in my boots like a pioneer,
> With the whole wide sky above me.

At one time in the American West, boots worn by the deceased often were nailed or tied to the wooden or stone cross over the deceased's grave. A few unmarked, as well as several marked graves of gold miners and their families are in boothill at the South Pass City State Historic Site.

WHAT'S A SAGE CHICKEN?

The correct name of the chicken-like bird of Western North America is a sage grouse. It's also called sage hen or prairie hen. The large grayish grouse lives in open sagebrush country, and is identified by a black belly patch and spinelike tail feathers. Its flushing note sounds like *kuk kuk kuk*, but during the courtship display, male sage chickens make a popping sound.

The courtship of sage grouse, in late April and early May, in Wyoming is spectacular. While dancing, the male, much larger than the female, puffs out his white chest and exposes the yellow air sacs on his

95

neck, spreading his pointed tail feathers. Sage grouse is a favorite game bird, but the open season in late summer is for a limited time.

WHAT'S A FALSE FRONT?

It's a wooden structure with a square front extending beyond the ridge of the roof of a building to give the effect of another story. Years ago in Wyoming, as well as in other states in the West, false-fronted buildings were typical structures for stores on the main street. Both gold mining camps, Atlantic City and South Pass City, in Fremont County, still have a few buildings with false fronts. Western movies with scenes of frontier towns often show streets with false-fronted saloons and stores.

The Smith-Sherlock store, with the false front, is one of the 19th century pine buildings at the South Pass City State Historic Site. This gold mining camp, the first in the Territory of Wyoming, flourished in the late 1860s and early 1870s. Books about the region as well as horehound, licorice and old-fashioned rock candy are popular items sold at the store by the Friends of South Pass.

WHAT'S A BUCK AND RAIL?

It's a pole fence supported by a sawbuck or sawhorse, having X-shaped legs projecting above the crossbar. The picturesque pine or cedar fences enclose many Wyoming ranches that often have more than a thousand acres. There are many buck and rail fences in the Teton National Park as well as in other areas of Western Wyoming.

WHAT ARE HOGBACKS?

They are long, narrow, and somewhat steep hills. Another way to describe a hogback is that it is a ridge with a sharp summit and steeply sloping sides. There are hogbacks in many areas of this country besides Wyoming.

The sheep wagon (featured on the cover) is an original product of Wyoming, built in Rawlins about 1887. It is the forerunner of the modern mobile home.

WHAT'S A SHEEP WAGON?

It's not a four-wheeled horse-drawn vehicle used to transport sheep. A sheep wagon is an enclosed canvas or metal-covered wagon on a wide wood base, with steel-rimmed wooden or rubber wheels. It's the sheepherder's home on the open range while he tends bands of sheep.

The interior of this one-room abode has a double bed, a built-in table that slides under the heavy wooden frame, which holds the mattress in place. It also has low, box-like cupboards that double as benches, a small four-plate iron stove with an oven, as well as shelves nailed to the rounded stays over which the canvas or metal top is placed.

The herder generally lives in the covered sheep wagon year-round, and most often his only companion is his faithful sheep dog, who guards the woollies from predators.

Not too many years ago, thousands of sheep grazed in Wyoming's sagebrush and grassy plains. There were also many sheep wagons among them.

Some claim that more sheep wagons are in town and city museums than on the prairies and foothills.

Prized as an antique collector's item, the sheep wagon, in many ways, is the forerunner of the mobile home. The first sheep wagon was built in Rawlins, in Carbon County, probably about 1887.

Sheep wagons have been the setting for activities other than herding. In the article, "Wyoming's Old, Unique Weddings," from the pamphlet, *Buffalo Bones,* Kathy Martinez, on the staff of the Wyoming State Archives, Museums, and Historical Department, wrote:

> The Sheep Queen of Wyoming, Miss Louisa Morrison, was united in holy matrimony on Jan. 19, 1901 with Ross Lambert. They were married in a sheep wagon near Casper at midnight.

Note: The author of this book, Lavinia Dobler, has a 1910 sheep wagon on her sagebrush-covered land near her six-sided solid log house that faces the Wind River Mountains.

WHAT'S A "HAPPY JACK?"

Years ago early settlers in Wyoming, and in other western states, made their lamps or lanterns from tin syrup cans, using homemade candles for light. These useful lanterns were commonly called "Happy Jacks."

WHAT'S A RANCH?

It's an extensive farm, especially in the American West, on which large herds of cattle, sheep or horses are raised. A ranch is also any large farm on which a particular crop or kind of animal is grown.

One of the largest ranches in Wyoming is the Yellowstone Ranch in the eastern part of Fremont County. In 1984 the ranch had about one million acres of deeded and federal land that was leased along the Sweetwater River. Yellowstone Ranch sprawls over a 100-mile area, according to Fremont County records in the courthouse at Lander. Formerly owned by the McIntosh family, William, Virginia, Jennifer and Joe, the large ranch was sold in 1977 to four men, who then sold it to the Yellowstone Ranch Company.

The McIntosh family have been ranchers for years in the Sweetwater area.

According to legend Indian hunters chased a huge white buffalo into Bull Lake that is also known as "The Lake that Roars." This glacier-fed body of water is on the Wind River Reservation in Fremont County.

WYOMING'S INDIAN LEGENDS

THE LEGEND OF "THE LAKE THAT ROARS"

Shoshone hunters were excited one early spring morning, countless moons ago, when they saw a huge, white buffalo grazing among the dark brown bison near the glacier-fed lake in the Wind River Mountains.

It was the first time they had ever had the chance to shoot a white bull, rare among the large, hoofed mammals with curved horns.

With mocassined feet the expert hunters, armed with bows and arrows, kicked their spotted ponies, and shouting wildly, raced toward the herd. They were determined to separate the white buffalo, with long shaggy hair on its broad shoulders, from the other bison.

The frightened bull lowered his massive head and dashed into the lake. In his attempt to get away from his pursuers, the white buffalo became exhausted, sank into the cold water and drowned.

During below-zero weather, the wind whips the snow-covered blocks of ice on Bull Lake, lifting the frozen masses and dropping them. The noise sounds like a prolonged roar. Many Shoshone Indians' explanation is that the white buffalo's spirit is roaring with anger.

Bull Lake, on the Wind River Reservation in Fremont County, is often called "The Lake that Roars."

THE LEGEND OF WIND RIVER CANYON

More than a hundred years ago, a young Shoshone chieftain and his sweetheart, whose long flowing hair was the color of obsidian, were walking along the winding river at the head of the many-colored Wind River Canyon in the Owl Creek Mountains. Suddenly the wind whisked an eagle feather from the girl's shining hair. Fascinated, the lovers watched the almost weightless object sail northward.

Later the wind dropped the feather on red earth beyond the rocky gorge, but the couple had no idea where the thunderbird's feather had gone.

When the lovers finally reached the area where they hoped to find the feather, to their great wonderment they watched a mist of cooling water vapor shoot out of the vermillion colored earth.

Puzzled, they looked at each other in awe, believing that the Great Spirit had led them to the mineral spring. They bathed in the warm water and then returned to the Shoshone camp to tell their people about the odd-smelling mineral spring.

The Shoshone families took down the many poles that supported their tepees made from buffalo hides, and set up a campsite near the spring.

Shoshone tribal members often boasted that their warriors and braves, who bathed in that mineral spring and others nearby, had greater physical strength and endurance than the Indian men from other tribes. Some people still claim that if a feather is released at the head of the chasm near Boysen Dam, it will float north toward the spring.

Wind River Canyon is one of the few chasms in Wyoming with a legend. At one time Shoshone Indians hunted and camped in the wilderness by the glacier-fed river. A portion of the canyon is on the Wind River Reservation, the home of the Shoshone and Arapaho Indians.

THE LEGEND OF LAKE DE SMET

One summer day, long ago, Little Moon, a handsome Indian brave of the Crow Tribe, and his true love Star Dust, arranged to meet that afternoon at their favorite tryst by the edge of the glacier-fed lake in the Big Horn Mountains.

The Crow maiden, with long black braided hair, was not only lovely in every way, but her brown eyes sparkled whenever she was with her beloved.

Later that day Little Moon sat by the lake, the blue-green water glimmering in the sunlight. While waiting for Star Dust, he saw the face of a young woman in the water. He not only was attracted to her, he thought she was the most beautiful Indian maiden he had ever seen. She smiled as though she were beckoning him to join her.

Just as Little Moon started to jump into the lake, his true love, Star Dust, touched his arm. Turning quickly around and scowling, he pushed her away, demanding that she return to their village. But when he turned back to face the sun shining on the water, eager to again admire the smiling face in the lake, it had disappeared.

The next morning Star Dust's body was found on the edge of the lake. Heartbroken, because his favorite daughter had drowned, legend has it that Star Dust's warrior father bound Little Moon to a huge boulder and left him to watch for the maiden the young brave thought he had seen in the lake.

THE BEARS AT DEVILS TOWER

The Sioux people called the stone obelisk, formed by lava, *Mato Tipe*, meaning Bear Lodge. It is said that Sitting Bull, victorious chieftain in the battle of the Little Bighorn, "made medicine" at the tower, getting the gods' promise of victory in one of the chief's most challenging campaigns.

In the Sioux version of Devils Tower, three Indian maidens were gathering wild flowers when they saw bears ready to attack them. So they ran to the huge boulder to escape from the dangerous animals. The gods, who realized that the Indian maidens were in great danger, caused the rock to rise high above the ground.

The bears tried to climb the boulder, but slowly the solid mass of stone rose higher and higher towards the sky. The bears, even with their strong claws could not hang onto the rock. One by one they fell to the ground and were killed.

With the flowers the Indian girls had gathered, they braided them into a long rope and then slid down the tower. The Sioux people claim that the marks on the rock wall were made by the bears' strong claws. There are other interesting legends about Devils Tower.

THE MEDICINE WHEEL MYSTERY

If there were ever any legends about the medicine wheel, the mysterious, prehistoric shrine or altar probably was built "before the light came," to the people of long ago, "who had no iron."

Archeologists, who have studied the wheel-like formation, continue to be puzzled and mystified. They have no clues to tell them what ancient Indian tribe constructed the shrine or when it was formed. They believe, however, that the primitive people probably were sun worshippers.

The Medicine Wheel, almost 250 feet in circumference, is located west of the city of Sheridan in the northern part of Wyoming, at the top of the Big Horn Mountains.

The three-foot-high central cairn of slate and stone probably represents the sun. Then from the center or hub, resembling spokes in a wheel, are 28 rocks which may be symbolic of the twenty-eight lunar days. There are six medicine tepees circling the perimeter of the wheel that may symbolize the planets. The bleached buffalo skull faces toward the early morning sun. The buffalo has always had deep significance for the Plains Indians.

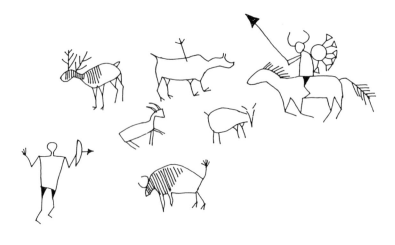

Figures like these were drawn long ago by people who hunted in Wilderness Wyoming.

ARTS IN THE
FORTY-FOURTH STATE

WHO WERE WYOMING'S
EARLIEST ARTISTS?

Indian artists used crude, primitive tools to draw or cut symbolic figures and animals on rocks and cliffs, as well as in caves and rock shelters. Pictographs and petroglyths are found in many areas of the state, including Castle Gardens, located about forty miles east of Riverton in Fremont County.

WHAT WERE WYOMING'S FIRST BOOKS?

The first books printed in the Wyoming wilderness were Indian vocabularies. The Army Press at Fort Laramie in 1868 printed *The Dictionary of the Sioux Language,* a pamphlet with thirty-three pages.

Then in 1868 the Freeman Brothers, Leigh R. and Fred K., of Green River City, printed *A Vocabulary of the Snake, or Sho-Sho-Nay Dialect* by Joseph A. Gebrow, interpreter.

WHICH PEAK IN THE TETON RANGE
IS NAMED FOR A WESTERN ARTIST?

Thomas Moran, born in England in 1837, was seven years old when his family came to the United States. Many years later Moran did some of his finest paintings in Wyoming. He accompanied F. V. Hayden's expedition to the Yellowstone region in 1871, the year before the scenic area was made a national park. From sketches of this trip, Moran painted the large study, "The Grand Canyon of the Yellowstone," which was purchased by the U.S. Congress.

Because of Moran's contributions to the West, Mount Moran, the fourth tallest peak in the Grand Tetons, was named for him. In the early part of this century, a tourist village near the dam at Jackson Lake, the second largest lake in Wyoming, was called Moran. At Moran Junction in northwestern Wyoming, the highway to the north leads to Jackson Lake Lodge, Colter Bay, and Yellowstone National Park. The highway to the south of Moran Junction leads to Grand Teton National Park and the mountainous town of Jackson.

WHAT TYPE OF 19TH CENTURY BUILDING WAS TYPICAL OF THE REMINGTON ERA?

The sod-roof, chink-log construction was typical of houses and barns on ranches and towns in 1890, when Wyoming was admitted as a state. The structures were also the type of building popular when Frederic Remington was living in the West.

Remington worked as a cowboy, scout and sheepherder in the mountains and prairies. Born in Canton, New York in 1861, he was not only a painter, he was also a gifted sculptor, illustrator and writer.

Remington's subjects were drawn primarily from life on the Western plains, show horses, cowboys, Indians and soldiers in action. His paintings, exciting portrayals of the West, have been extensively reproduced in prints.

Before Remington died in 1909, at the age of forty-eight, he had completed some 2,700 drawings. Replicas of his twenty-three bronzes are in many collections and museums in the United States, including the Buffalo Bill Historical Center in Cody.

Remington's studio in New Rochelle, New York, the gift of Lawrence Rockefeller, is on permanent display at the Buffalo Bill Historical Center. The Center is the finest museum in Wyoming, and ranks among the best in the nation.

WHERE IS THE NOVEL, *WILD WIND, WILD WATER*, SET IN WYOMING?

The town of Riverton on the Wind River in Fremont County is the setting for the first historical novel to be written about the 1906 government land lottery. The author, Lavinia Dobler, used the name Wind River instead of Riverton, because of the town's location near the river, the most important waterway in that section of Wyoming, east of the Wind River Mountains.

The book is written about the struggle the author's parents, George and Grace Sessions Dobler, both homesteaders, encountered, along with other early Riverton settlers, who attempted to get water for the arid land.

During the first land lottery in Wyoming, Dobler's number "111" was drawn from a metal box on Saturday, August 4, 1906 on Main Street in Lander. He immediately filed on the claim of 160 acres and began proving up on his homestead, which was located in site of Griffey Hill, a few miles west of town.

Wyoming Governor Fenimore Chatterton had envisioned a prosperous agricultural community in Riverton if canals were built. Banker and salt magnate of Chicago, Joy Morton, who represented the Wyoming Central Irrigation Company, and the state engineer Clarence Johnson signed the contract on August 1, 1906, giving the company the right to build laterals on the sagebrush land north of the Wind River that had been formerly part of the Wind River Reservation.

The campus of Central Wyoming College was the former homestead of pioneer lawyer and judge George F. Dobler. The town of Riverton was first called Wadsworth, for the Indian agent, but later the name was changed to Riverton, the largest town in Fremont County.

The novel was among those selected to appear on the 1984 full-color Wyoming literary map, published by the University of Wyoming.

DOES WYOMING HAVE A STATE SONG?

The lyric, "Wyoming," was written by Charles E. Winter of Casper, with music by George E. Knapp, and adopted by the thirty-third legislature in 1955 as the state song.

Winter, author of several historical novels about Wyoming, wrote the poem the summer of 1903, and Earle R. Clemens composed the music. The song was introduced that summer at the State Industrial Association convention in Sheridan. The following year, 1904, the song was presented at the World's Fair in St. Louis.

Savilla King, paternal aunt of former president Gerald Ford, then a young girl whose home was in Casper, sang "Wyoming" on "Wyoming Day" at the Portland, Oregon fair, July 10, 1905. The daughter of the pioneer entrepreneur of central Wyoming, C. H. King, Savilla was dressed in a glamorous white Parisian evening gown with a long train.

In 1920, George E. Knapp, professor of music at the University of Wyoming, wrote music in march tempo for Winter's poem and arranged it for group and chorus singing.

The words of the first stanza and chorus are:

> In the far and mighty West,
> Where the crimson sun seeks rest,
> There's a growing splendid state
> that lies above.
> On the breast of this great land;
> Where the massive Rockies stand,
> There's Wyoming young and strong,
> the State I love!

Wyoming, Wyoming! Land of the sunlight clear!
Wyoming, Wyoming! Land that we hold so dear!
Wyoming, Wyoming! Precious art thou and
   thine!
Wyoming, Wyoming! Beloved State of Mine!

*Built during the late Nineteenth Century, the Sheridan Inn is
famous for its sixty-nine gables.*

WHICH WYOMING INN DID RIPLEY CALL
"THE HOUSE OF SIXTY-NINE GABLES"?

Robert Ripley called the Sheridan Inn, built during
the 1890s on the outskirts of Sheridan, "The House
of Sixty-Nine Gables." Located south of the Big
Horn Mountains, the Inn has many vertical triangles. In fact, the sixty-nine gable design makes the
building unique as well as attractive.

111

The large wooden structure, with windows in the sixty-nine vertical triangles called gables, has a wide porch that runs along the front of the dark brown building and the south side.

Costing $75,000, Sheridan Inn was built by the Burlington and Missouri Railroad (now known as the Burlington Northern) and the Sheridan Land Company. Thomas R. Kimball, architect from Omaha, designed the hotel to resemble an old country inn he had admired while visiting Scotland.

When the striking and unusual Sheridan Inn opened, many claimed that it was one of the finest hotels between Chicago and San Francisco.

Dressed in elegant clothes, Colonel William Frederick Cody, better known as "Buffalo Bill" Cody, had the honor of leading the grand march, Sunday evening, June 18, 1893. He owned Sheridan Inn between 1894-1896. For years the Inn was the center of social life not only for the town of Sheridan, but the surrounding areas.

Wealthy ranch owners, in black suits with tails, and women in colorful silk and satin evening gowns often danced the Virginia reel and the schottische (the round dance in three-quarter time).

Distinguished visitors who stayed at the Sheridan Inn were three presidents: Theodore Roosevelt, William Howard Taft and Herbert Hoover; Calamity Jane (whose real name was Martha Canary), Charles Russell, artist of the West; and Ernest Hemingway, famous author; as well as generals, including John J. Pershing, whose wife was Frances Warren of Cheyenne. She was the daughter of Francis E. Warren, the first elected state governor of Wyoming in 1890. At the time of his death in 1929, Senator Warren had served Wyoming in the upper house of Congress for thirty-seven years, the longest service record, at that time, in the U.S. Senate.

In 1964 Sheridan Inn was recognized as a National Historic Landmark. However the next year it was not operated as a hotel. Then in 1967, Mrs. Neltje Kings purchased the fine historic building, and it reopened officially in 1969. (Source: *Wyoming, A Guide to Historic Places*, Wyoming Recreation Commission).

WHOSE PHOTOGRAPHS CONVINCED CONGRESS TO SET ASIDE YELLOWSTONE?

Photographs taken by William H. Jackson during the 1870s while he was a member of the F. V. Hayden expedition, helped to convince Congressmen that Yellowstone should be set aside as a national park.

Born in Keeseville, New York in 1843, Jackson is recognized as one of the best early photographers of the American West. As a young man he devoted his life to recording the scenic grandeur and historic sites of the West. He settled in Omaha, Nebraska in 1868.

Among many photographic studies, Jackson took pictures of the building of the Union Pacific Railroad across southern Wyoming. When photographing the peaks of the Tetons and other points in the northwestern part of the state, he and his men used horse-drawn wagons to carry cameras and other gear, but later switched to mules, one Jackson called Molly.

The artist took photographs of South Pass City in the early 1870s when the gold mining camp was one of the largest in the territory. He climbed a rocky point, east of South Pass City and took a photo of the wooden buildings that lined the main street. The photograph is considered one of the best ever taken of the town during the boom period.

Impressed with his artistic ability, state officials commissioned Jackson to take a series of photographs of Wyoming scenery to be exhibited at the 1893 Columbian Exposition in Chicago.

WHO ARE "WYOMING'S MUSICAL AMBASSADORS?"

The state legislature officially proclaimed the Casper Troopers "Wyoming's Musical Ambassadors" in 1967.

The Troopers also received the Veterans of Foreign Wars National Title the year before, and placed second in the World Open Championship. In 1965 the drum and bugle corps won the World Open and took many titles during their eastern state tour.

James E. Jones, founder and director, organized the Casper Troopers, a group of boys and girls ranging in age from 12 to 21. According to the *Wyoming Blue Book*, Volume III:

> Jones, a building contractor, had the theory that the corps would be an excellent character building activity for Casper young people. The dedicated Troopers work hard and practice rigid self discipline. This has produced a unique 130-member marching unit that has captured world honors and has become a source of pride to all of Wyoming.

WHICH ACTOR WAS A CLOSE FRIEND OF MANY WYOMING NATIVE AMERICANS?

Cowboy Tim McCoy made his acting debut in 1922 with 500 Arapaho, Shoshone and Bannock Indians he recruited for the movie, "The Covered Wagon." The movie was the first of several filmed on the Wind River Reservation.

A respected member of the Arapaho tribe, Goes-in-Lodge, adopted McCoy as his blood brother. They remained close friends for many years. Two sons of Chief Washakie, Dick and Charlie, were also good friends of Tim McCoy. They acted in many films with the movie star.

Two Arapaho men, Tom Crispin and Mike Goggles taught McCoy the sign language, and the Goggles family, besides appearing in several Hollywood movies, were in demand at many events to display their Indian dancing. By erecting their tepee and performing, they assisted McCoy in the early establishment of the famous "Frontier Days" celebration, held annually in Cheyenne the last full week in July.

WHICH CELEBRATED SHAKESPEAREAN ACTOR PLAYED "HAMLET" IN CHEYENNE?

Edwin Booth played the title role in the Shakespearean production of "Hamlet" in 1887 at the Cheyenne Opera House. The playbills were printed in silk as well as on fine paper.

Francis E. Warren, wealthy cattleman, was serving as treasurer of Wyoming Territory in 1882 when he built the opera house.

Edwin Booth was the brother of the actor and Confederate sympathizer, John Wilkes Booth, who assassinated President Abraham Lincoln on Good Friday, April 14, 1865 at Ford's Theatre in Washington, D.C.

WHICH WYOMING JOURNALIST WAS KNOWN AS ONE OF THE BEST 19TH CENTURY WITS?

Edgar Wilson Nye, better known as Bill Nye, was born in Maine. He lived in Wisconsin for twenty-four years before he migrated to Wyoming Territory in 1876.

Nye was admitted to the Wyoming bar and became a judge. He also edited the Laramie *Boomerang* for three years, a newspaper he founded and used to print his humorous comments and yarns about frontier life.

Collections of his works appeared in *Bill Nye and Boomerang* (1881), *Forty Liars and Other Lies* (1882), and *Baled Hay* (1884).

The humorist moved to New York City in 1896 and wrote for the *World* newspaper. He also gave lyceum and recitals, some of them with poet James Whitcomb Riley.

WHO HAS A COLLECTION OF INDIAN DRESSES?

For years Jeri Greeves, a Kiowa and former member of the Wyoming Council on the Arts, sold Indian arts and crafts at the Fort Washakie Trading Post on North Fork Road in the Wind River Indian Reservation.

There are over fifty costumes in Jeri Greeves' collection of Native American wearing apparel. Her first Kiowa dresses were acquired while working as a teenager at the Southern Plains Indian Museum at Anadarko, Oklahoma.

One striking costume Mrs. Greeves models is a South Arapaho ghost dance dress. Her great-grandmother wore the dress during the late Nineteenth Century when ghost dances were still practiced. The Paiute messiah Wovoka of Nevada in 1889 introduced the ghost dance as a religious ceremony.

Mrs. Greeves often purchased unusual Indian costumes from members of other tribes who traveled to the Wind River Reservation to dance in the annual summer pow-wows.

WHOSE SCULPTURE WAS GIVEN TO THE QUEEN DURING THE U.S. BICENTENNIAL?

Harry Jackson's famous bronze "The Two Champions," was this country's gift to Elizabeth, reigning queen of England, in 1976, during the U.S. Bicentennial celebration. Jackson is recognized as an outstanding sculptor of the American West. Jackson's bronze of Sacajawea, the Indian guide-interpreter on the Lewis and Clark Expedition, is in the Buffalo Bill Historical Museum in Cody, as well as on the campus of Central Wyoming College in Riverton.

Jackson has also done a striking bronze of John Wayne, movie actor. That bronze is in the Arts Center lobby at Central Wyoming College.

WHEN WAS THE ST. STEPHENS INDIAN MISSION HERITAGE CENTER DEDICATED?

The Heritage Center was dedicated on May 20, 1984, highlighting the 100th anniversary of St. Stephens Indian Mission on the Wind River Reservation, a few miles south of Riverton.

Arapaho collections include the old saddle used by Francis Setting Eagle, one of the early students in 1892. The collection of the *Wind River Rendezvous* magazines is also on display. These publications often in full color, are probably the most popular source of information about the reservation and the life of the Shoshone and Arapaho Indians available today, according to the Reverend Anthony J. Short, S.J., the first director of the Heritage Center.

Long before white men came into the wilderness now known as Wyoming, Indians were creating artistic drawings.

WHO WAS APPOINTED WYOMING'S POET LAUREATE IN 1987?

Governor Mike Sullivan, in 1987, appointed Charles Levendosky, of Casper, as Wyoming's Poet Laureate. This well-known poet is editorial page editor and columnist for the Casper *Star-Tribune*. He was awarded the H.L. Mencken Award by the Free Press Association in 1988. Levendosky has published several volumes of poetry and has given readings to large audiences in many cities throughout the United States.

In May, 1990, Levendosky gave an important talk in Sheridan on what the First Amendment to the U.S. Constitution means. He reminded those who were present at the meeting that American citizens must be very vigilant in protecting the First Amendment rights. The program was presented by the Sheridan Arts Council and the Wyoming Council on the Arts.

WYOMING ON FILM

WHAT ARE SOME OF THE FILMS WITH WYOMING AS THE SETTING?

Steven R. Peck, an authority on films, is Associate Publisher of the Riverton *Ranger* and Editor of *Extra*, the special entertainment section that appears weekly in the newspaper. Peck wrote: "Hollywood hasn't ignored Wyoming over the years. Many feature films and television programs have been filmed in the state or have used Wyoming as a setting for their stories." Peck's list includes 60 films.

WYOMING ROUNDUP (1904)
This almost certainly qualifies as the earliest movie ever filmed in the state. The silent western was shot in and around Rock River.

CHARGE OF THE LIGHT BRIGADE (1912)
Thomas Edison's film company came to the Cheyenne area to shoot this silent picture with a historical theme.

HANDSOME JIM SHERWOOD (1917)
Legendary swashbuckler Douglas Fairbanks starred in this silent action picture, which used several locations near Laramie as backdrops for Fairbanks and friends.

BEFORE THE WHITE MAN CAME (1917)
Another silent, this one with an Indian theme, was shot near Sheridan.

HEART OF THE WILD (1918)

Filmed near Cody, this picture starred Elsie Ferguson, an actress of silent movie fame who has largely been forgotten today.

THE HELLCAT (1918)

This film caused a stir for its racy title. The Goldwyn Picture Co. filmed it near Cody.

THE DUKE OF CHIMNEY BUTTE (1919)

Silent-movie audiences had a voracious appetite for western locales. Fred Stone starred in this scenic silent that was filmed near Cheyenne and Pine Bluffs.

NAN OF THE NORTH (1912)

Yellowstone National Park provided scenic locales for this tale starring Ann Little, another little-remembered silent player.

THE COWBOY AND THE LADY (1922)

Early cowboy star Tom Moore wooed Mary Miles Minter in this western filmed in Jackson Hole.

THE DANGEROUS TRAIL (1923)

A regional film company, Rocky Mountain Productions, shot this feature in and around Cheyenne.

THE LAWLESS MEN (1923)

Shot near Lusk, this western starred Neal Hart, who also served as producer.

THE THUNDERING HERD (1924)

Rugged cowboy actor Tom Holt starred with Lois Wilson in this production filmed near Cody by Famous Players Lasky Co., one of Hollywood's most successful early studios.

THE PONY EXPRESS (1925)
Wallace Beery, destined for a long career as a character actor, makes one of his earliest appearances in this western shot near Cheyenne.

THREE BAD MEN (1925)
Another western, this one starring George O'Brien and featuring numerous locales near Jackson.

WARPAINT (1926)
Filmed at Fort Washakie, this western featured authentic Arapaho Indians such as Goes-in-Lodge, Bad Teeth, Night Horse and George Wallowingbull with Tim McCoy, one of the biggest western stars of the silent era.

CHEYENNE (1928)
The title tells where this western adventure was filmed. Famous cowboy actor Ken Maynard starred.

THE VIRGINIAN (1929)
The first of two versions of the Owen Wister novel was among the very first talking Westerns ever made. It stars a very young Gary Cooper, and is directed by Victor Fleming, who later directed "Gone with the Wind" and "The Wizard of Oz," among others.

BIG TRAIL (1930)
John Wayne, still years away from stardom, appeared with Tyrone Power in this western filmed near Jackson by the Fox-Movietone Co. The film was shot in the then-pioneering 70-m format called "Grandeur."

YELLOWSTONE (1936)
A group of treasure hunters scours Yellowstone National Park for some loot stashed there years before. Andy Devine and Ralph Morgan are among the stars.

WYOMING (1940)

Here's another routine Western, which stars character actor, Wallace Beery and his side-kick Leo Carrillo. Richard Thorpe directed the story of on-again and off-again friends.

BAD BASCOMB (1946)

Wallace Beery returned to Wyoming once again is this action-packed MGM Western filmed near Jackson. Marjorie Main and Maret O'Brien co-starred.

THE VIRGINIAN (1946)

Joel McCrea stars in the remake of the 1929 film. This one's not quite as good or famous as the original.

CHEYENNE (1947)

Raoul Walsh directed this western starring Dennis Morgan and Jane Wyman. It later was renamed "The Wyoming Kid."

WYOMING (1947)

"Wild Bill" Elliot stars with Vera Ralston and Gabby Hayes in this pretty good western drama that pairs off homesteaders and ranchers. Joseph Kane was the director.

WYOMING MAIL (1950)

The plot concerns a postal robbery in the old west. Stephen McNallay and Alexis Smith get top billing.

BIG SKY (1952)

Yet another western shot in Jackson Hole, this one starred Kirk Douglas as a fur trapper leading an expedition up the Missouri River. This fine film, directed by Howard Hawks, is an example of a picture that was shot in Wyoming but had its fictional setting elsewhere.

SHANE (1952)

One of the greatest westerns ever made, this George Stevens classic starred Alan Ladd, Jean Arthur and Jack Palance. Breathtaking Jackson Hole scenery abounds in this story of a gunfighter trying to put his past behind him.

WYOMING RENEGADES (1955)

This, unfortunately, is the worst of the films with Wyoming in the title. An ex-outlaw, played by Phil Carey, tries to go straight. Fred Sears was the director.

THE FAR HORIZONS (1955)

This tale of the Lewis and Clark expedition starred Charlton Heston and Fred MacMurray. It, too, was filmed near Jackson.

THE MAN FROM LARAMIE (1955)

Here's an exciting western featuring a standout performance by star James Stewart as a man from (you guessed it) out to avenge the death of his brother.

JUBAL (1956)

Glenn Ford, Ernest Borgnine and Rod Steiger topped the cast list for this unusual western adaptation of Shakespeare's "Othello." It was shot in Jackson Hole.

THE SHERIFF OF FRACTURED JAW (1959)

One of the last films directed by the great Raoul Walsh, this western spoof is based in the fictitious Wyoming town of Fractured Jaw. An Englishman is given the unenviable job as sheriff, and it makes for a few laughs. Kenneth More, Jayne Mansfield and Robert Morely are featured.

THIS IS AMERICA (1962)

This unusual film was the famous "Circle Vision" program at Disneyland for more than 20 years. The film, which was projected on a huge, 360-degree movie screen, featured the Teton Range and scenes of a Wyoming cattle ranch.

SPENCER'S MOUNTAIN (1963)

This was a film version of the story that later became the long-running television series "The Waltons." Henry Fonda starred as the head of a large Wyoming family. It was filmed near Jackson.

CHEYENNE AUTUMN (1964)

A true "all-star" cast graced this western directed by John Ford, one of the greatest American filmmakers. This was Ford's last film. It starred Richard Widmark, James Stewart, Edward G. Robinson and many others. It was filmed near Fort Laramie.

THE UNEXPECTED MRS. POLLIFAX (1969)

Filmed near Jackson, this little-seen picture starred Darren McGavin and Rosalind Russell.

THE WILD COUNTRY (1969)

Based on the "Little Britches" book series, this is the story of a pioneer family in Wyoming. Vera Miles, Steve Forrest and Ron Howard are the stars. Shot in Teton and Fremont counties, the film borrowed the name of real-life rancher Ab Cross for one of its characters.

THE HELLFIGHTERS (1969)

One of the biggest hits of 1969 was this story of the famous oil-rig firefighters headed by Red Adair. John Wayne and Jim Hutton starred, with much of the action filmed in Casper.

THE CHEYENNE SOCIAL CLUB (1970)

This Western comedy teamed James Stewart and Henry Fonda for the only time in their careers. The drifter (Stewart) is called to Cheyenne to take over his dead brother's business. This engaging comedy was directed by Gene Kelly.

RAGE (1972)

George C. Scott directed and starred in the modern-day tale about a Rawlins area rancher who is exposed to nerve gas along with his young son. His rage comes when neither government nor miliary authorities will help him. You'll recognize some of the scenery around Baroil, Wyoming.

BADLANDS (1973)

Director Terrence Malick adapted the true story of the Charles Starkweather murder case from the 1950s for the screen. A madman, played by Martin Sheen, killed a number of innocent people and fled to the barren Wyoming badlands near Douglas, where he was apprehended.

THE MAN WHO LOVED CAT DANCING (1973)

Burt Reynolds, Sarah Miles, Lee J. Cobb, and George Hamilton starred in this enjoyable Western film concerning a defiant woman who takes up with a bunch of hard-nosed outlaws. The film is based in Wyoming and features Jay Silverheels, who played Tonto on the popular "Lone Ranger" TV series. The film's director was Richard Sarafian.

CLOSE ENCOUNTERS OF THE THIRD KIND (1977)

One of the classics of modern cinema, Steven Spielberg's famous story of visitors from space uses Wyoming's Devils Tower near Moorcroft, as its focal point. Richard Dreyfuss, Teri Garr and Melinda Dillon are the stars.

THE MOUNTAIN MEN (1979)

Charlton Heston and Brian Keith play a couple of Wyoming trappers and traders in this Columbia Pictures release filmed in Teton and Fremont Counties.

HEARTLAND (1979)

Based on "The Diary of a Woman Homesteader" by Elinore Pruitt Stewart, this film chronicles the struggles of a young woman and her authoritarian employer, a Scotsman, in the wild of Wyoming, in the Burnt Fork area, circa 1910. Rip Torn and Conchata Farrell starred.

THE PURSUIT OF D.B. COOPER (1980)

When the producers looked for a location to shoot this fictional account of a real-life airline hijacker on the run, they picked Wyoming. Treat Williams and Robert Duvall star, with Jackson Hole as their backdrop.

HEAVEN'S GATE (1980)

This film is perhaps the most famous flop in film history. "Heaven's Gate" has come to symbolize filmmaking extravagance. A dramatized account of the famous Johnson County range war, the film was directed by Michael Cimino, an Oscar winner for the film "The Deer Hunter" in 1978. The film, which almost single-handedly destroyed United Artists Studios, stars Kris Kristofferson, Cristopher Walken and Isabel Huppert.

ANY WHICH WAY YOU CAN (1980)

Clint Eastwood filmed the second half the sequel to "Every Which Way But Loose" in Jackson. The film features a memorable fist-fight in downtown Jackson, and many locals appeared on screen. Unfortunately, the two films often are shown in a poorly-edited-combined-version on television.

TOM HORN (1980)

Steve McQueen played Tom Horn, the legendary prairie lawman who was revered by some, hated by others. Many scenes of the famous bounty hunter's life were shot in Wyoming, but the film's photography is its redeeming factor. Directed by William Wiard, it was Steve McQueens' next to the last film before he died.

ENDANGERED SPECIES (1981)

A New York police officer investigates cattle mutilations on a western ranch. Robert Urich and JoBeth Williams play the lead roles in this film, shot near Buffalo.

STAR TREK: THE MOTION PICTURE (1982)

Parts of this blockbuster were filmed in Yellowstone National Park. William Shatner, Leonard Nimoy and the rest of the starship Enterprise crew are featured.

SUPERGIRL (1984)

Aerial footage used in the depiction of flight by Supergirl were shot near Jeffrey City. Helen Slater played the girl of steel.

ROCKY IV (1985)

Wintry Jackson Hole stood in for wintry Russia in this third sequel to the Oscar-winning original. Sylvester Stallone sprinted up one of the Tetons in a training scene. Not very realistic, but memorable all the same.

WILD HORSES (1985)

This CBS television movie was shot near Sheridan. Kenny Rogers, Richard Farnsworth and Pam Dawber starred.

DREAM WEST (1985)

Jackson and Gillette were among the settings used in the shooting of this CBS television mini-series starring Richard Chamberlain.

PRISON (1987)

This strange horror film concerned the spirit of an executed man coming to haunt the prison where the execution took place. The Wyoming State Penitentiary in Rawlins was the setting.

INTO THE HOMELAND (1987)

Powers Boothe and C. Thomas Howell starred in this Home Box Office film shot on location near Buffalo and Sheridan.

THE WRONG GUYS (1987)

Comedians Louie Anderson and Richard Belzer head the cast of this manic caper about, of all things, a Cub Scout reunion near Jackson.

POW WOW HIGHWAY (1987)

George Harrison's Handmade Films produced this unusual and memorable film about a Cheyenne Indian man on a road trip to New Mexico. Most of the film was shot near Sheridan, where it had its world premiere.

GHOSTS CAN'T DO IT (1989)

Sex symbol Bo Derek and veteran actor Anthony Quinn star in this comedy filmed in and around Jackson.

ALWAYS (1989)

Steven Spielberg's visually breath-taking tale of forest firefighters took some of its spectacular fire footage from the 1988 Yellowstone National Park forest fires.

BIBLIOGRAPHY

Allyn, Mary J.; *Twentieth Century Pioneering: Our Frontier Days Experiences at Riverton, Wyoming* (Riverton: 1956).

Beach, Cora M.; *Women of Wyoming*, in two volumes, (Casper: S. E. Boyer & Co., 1927-1929).

Bonney, Orrin H. and Lorraine; *Guide to the Wyoming Mountains and Wilderness Areas* (Denver: a Sage book published by Alan Swallow, 1960).

Burgess, Florence F.; Dobler, Lavinia; Vincent-Haas, Geraldine; Williamson, Rosemary; editors, *Family Stories, Riverton, Wyoming 1906-1981;* (Riverton: Riverton Senior Citizens Center, 1981).

Casper Star-Tribune; (Casper: 1984), selected newspaper articles.

Coutant, C. G.; *The History of Wyoming*, (Laramie: Caplin, Spafford & Mathison, 1899).

Coutant, C. G.; *Progressive Men of Wyoming* (Chicago: A. W. Bowen & Co., 1903). Coutant is believed to have prepared this large volume.

Craighead, John J., Craighead, Frank C. Jr., and Davis, Ray A.; *A Field Guide to Rocky Mountain Wildflowers* (Boston: Houghton Miflin Co., 1963).

Dobler, Lavinia; *Wild Wind, Wild Water*, (Casper: Misty Mountain Press, 1983).

Drury, Clifford M.; *First White Women Over the Rockies*, 3 volumes (Glendale: The Arthur H. Clark Co., 1963-1966).

Gowans, Fred R.; *Rocky Mountain Rendezvous: A History of the Fur Trade Rendezvous 1825-1840*, (Provo, Utah: Brigham Young University Press, 1975).

Grant, Bruce; *The Cowboy Encyclopedia: The Old and New West from the Open Range to the Dude Ranch*, (Chicago: Rand McNally & Co., 1951).

Hall, Charles; *Documents of Wyoming Heritage*, (Cheyenne: Wyoming Bicentennial Commission, 1976).

Howard, Robert West; *The South Pass Story*, (New York: G. P. Putnam's Sons, 1968).

Jost, Loren, editor; *Exploring Fremont County History*, Vol. I, Vol. 11 and Vol. III, (Riverton: Central Wyoming College, 1982, 1983, 1985).

Jost, Loren, editor; *Riverton, the Early Days: A History of Riverton, Wyoming*, as told by contemporary newspaper accounts during the years 1906-1953, (Riverton: compiled by Lavinia Dobler and other members of the Riverton Historical Research Committee, 1981).

Kouris, Diana Allen: *The Romantic and Notorious History of Brown's Park*, (Greybull: Wolverine Gallery, 1988).

Larson, T. A.; *History of Wyoming*, second edition, revised, (Lincoln: University of Nebraska Press, 1978).

Linford, Velma; *Wyoming: Frontier State*, (Denver: The Old West Publishing Co., 1947).

Mead, Jean; *Casper County, Wyoming's Heartland*, (Boulder: Pruett Publishing Co., 1987).

Mead, Jean; *Wyoming in Profile*, (Boulder: Pruett Publishing Co., 1982).

Mitchell, Finis; *Wind River Trails*, (Salt Lake City: Wasatch Publishing, Inc., 1975).

Murray, Larry, director of Curriculum Development Workshop, *The Wind River Reservation: Yesterday and Today.*

Peck, Robert, publisher; *(Riverton Ranger):* specific articles from the newspaper in the 1980s.

Pence, Mary Lou, and Homsher, Lola M.; *The Ghost Towns of Wyoming,* (New York: Hastings House, 1956).

Roberts, Phil, editor; *More Buffalo Bones,* (Cheyenne: Wyoming State Archives, Museums and Historical Department, 1982).

Sherlock, James L.; *South Pass and Its Tales,* (Basin: Saddlebag Books, 1987).

Short, Anthony, S. J., editor; *Wind River Rendezvous* (magazine), Vol. XIV, No. 2, April, May, June, 1984 (Riverton: St. Stephens Indian Mission Foundation, 1984).

Spring, Agnes Wright, and Linford, Dee: *Wyoming: A Guide to its History, Highways, and People* (New York: Oxford University Press, 1941). Compiled by the Writers Program of the Work Projects Administration in the State of Wyoming.

Sniffen, William, publisher; *Wyoming State Journal,* (Lander: 1984), articles by Tom Bell for Lander's 100th anniversary.

Thompson, Edith M. Schultz, and Thompson, William Leigh; *Beaver Dick: The Honor and the Heartbreak,* (Laramie: Jelm Mountain Press, 1981).

Trenholm, Virginia Cole, editor; *Wyoming Blue Book*, in three volumes. Reprint of Part I and Part II of *Wyoming Historical Blue Book*, by Marie Erwin, (Cheyenne: Wyoming State Archives and Historical Department, 1974). Volume I, *Acquisition of Land Through Territorial Days;* Volume II, *Statehood until 1943;* Volume III, 1976. *The Supplement* was compiled principally from data found in the State Archives and Historical Department.

Urbanek, Mae; *Ghost Trails of Wyoming*, (Boulder: Johnson Publishing Co., 1978).

Urbanek, Mae; *Wyoming Place Names*, (Missoula: Mountain Press Publishing Co., 1988).

Watts, Peter, *A Dictionary of the Old West, 1850-1900*, (New York: Alfred A. Knopf, 1977).

Western Writers of America; *The Women Who Made the West: Stories of Unsung Heroines of the American West*, (Doubleday & Co., Inc., 1980), introduction by Nellie Snyder Yost.

Wyoming Recreation Commission, *Wyoming Registry of Sites Enrolled in the National Register of Historic Sites*, (Cheyenne: Wyoming Recreation Commission).

Wyoming Recreation Commission; *Wyoming: A Guide to Historic Sites*, (Basin: Big Horn Publishers, 1976). Introduction by Paul H. Westedt, Director, Wyoming Recreation Commission.

Wyoming Writers, Roberta Cheney and Emmie D. Mygatt, editors; *This is Wyoming Listen...* contents contributed by members of Wyoming Writers, (Basin: Big Horn Books, 1977).

ABOUT THE AUTHOR-HISTORIAN

Lavinia Dobler is a Wyoming native, and with her sister Virginia, were the first twins born in the frontier town of Riverton in 1910. Her parents George and Grace Sessions Dobler were among pioneer homesteaders, who, in 1906, won 160-acre tracts of land in the government lottery. George Dobler, a lawyer, later served as a judge and state legislator from Fremont County. His homestead is now the site for Central Wyoming College and the Dobler Room was named for the family. Grace Dobler was one of the early teachers in the new town by the Wind River.

Lavinia was a news reporter, teacher, English supervisor in Puerto Rico, and research librarian for Scholastic Magazines and Books in New York City. Her young adult novel *A Business of Their Own*, about the organization Junior Achievement, won the Dodd-Mead "National Librarian Award" in 1957. She was honored by Wyoming Writers with the esteemed "Emmie Mygatt Award" in 1981. Lavinia received the Wyoming Council for the Humanities Award in 1988.

Among her three dozen books, she authored a number of reference and textbooks, including *Customs and Holidays Around the World, When Greatness Called: Stories of Courage in America, National Holidays Around the World* and the *Arrow Book of the United Nations*, a readable reference book about the world peace organization. The author's historical novel, *Wild Wind, Wild Water*, dramatizes the story of her parents' struggle, as well as other settlers, to get irrigation water to Riverton area homesteaders.

In 1986, Lavinia presented the plan to preserve the historic mountain man's 1838 Rendezvous Site on the Wind Rivers as Riverton's long-lasting legacy in celebration of the 1990 Wyoming Centennial.

INDEX

143